Bolton Davidheiser is a graduate of Swarthmore College (A.B.) and Johns Hopkins University (Ph.D.). He has held two research fellowships and served as Professor of Biology at Westmont College, Santa Barbara, California, and Professor of Biology at Biola College at La Mirada, California.

For eleven years he has contributed a monthly column in the *Kings Business,* "Science and the Bible." He has delivered several technical papers on Genetics, Science, and Creation for scholarly and research groups and associations.

Science
and The Bible

by
Bolton Davidheiser

BAKER BOOK HOUSE
Grand Rapids, Michigan

Library of Congress Catalog Card Number: 73-146116
Standard Book Number: 8010-2807-8

PHOTOLITHOPRINTED BY CUSHING - MALLOY, INC.
ANN ARBOR, MICHIGAN, UNITED STATES OF AMERICA
1971

Contents

1. The Greatness of God in Nature

Christians have been cautioned against attributing to the handiwork of God the wonders of nature because, it is said, as science finds explanations of natural phenomena God becomes, in a sense, smaller and smaller. But the Bible tells us that "The heavens declare the glory of God and the firmament showeth His handiwork" (Ps. 19:1), and that the heathen are without excuse for their idolatry because the evidence of the handiwork of God is so clear in nature (Rom. 1:20-23).

There is no need to be concerned about science displacing God. The more that is found out about the world of nature, the more marvellous the works of God are shown to be instead of less so.

Science has nothing to say about purpose. There is a tendency among scientists to ignore or even to dislike questions that involve purpose. Some years ago a scientist writing in a scientific magazine exhorted his fellow scientists not to use expressions implying purpose in nature. He says that teachers should avoid such statements as: Some plants store starch. They should use the word "accumulate" instead of "store," because the word "store" implies a purpose in providing for the future. He even went so far as to say that teachers should not say to their classes that hydrogen and oxygen combine to form water. They should say that hydrogen and oxygen combine *and* (not *to*) form water, so as to avoid the possible implication that there is purpose involved in this chemical reaction. He says this is not quibbling and that teachers need to be very careful to avoid implying purpose in nature. As is clear in the rest of his article, the reason for such zeal in avoiding attributing purpose to nature is to prevent attributing anything in nature to acts of God.

If the heathen in Paul's day were without excuse because the acts of God in nature were so evident, how much more are we without excuse with our greatly extended knowledge of these things!

There is an almost endless array of phenomena in nature that defy a mechanistic or evolutionary explanation. Some birds navigate by the stars when migrating, and birds raised from eggs inside a building where they have never seen the sky can orient toward their home position when shown an artificial sky representing a place on the earth where their species never goes.

Archer fish shoot drops of water with great accuracy at insects; but this feat cannot be attributed to "survival of the fittest," for this manner of capturing insects is only a hobby with them. When hungry they secure their food after the manner of other fish.

Mites which parasitize certain moths live in an ear of the moth, destroying it. But however much that ear of the moth becomes overcrowded by the increase in the mite family or by additional mites coming aboard, they will not enter the other ear. If both ears were destroyed the moth and mites together would fall easy prey to the bats; for, when the moth hears the high-frequency squeaks of the bat, it performs gyrating-avoiding reactions.

The bombardier beetle produces chemicals which mix to form a violent explosion in the face of its enemy, but the explosion does not occur prematurely and it does not blow the beetle apart. It works right the first time, and it always has done so in the ancestry of every living bombardier beetle.

Honey bees that have found a new source of nectar communicate to other bees in the hive the direction and distance, even though they have returned by a circuitous route.

A mold growing in the ground develops microscopic loops only when certain minute worms are present in the soil. If a worm touches the outside of a loop nothing happens. But if it touches the inside of a loop the loop constricts in a fraction of a second, holding the worm tightly. The mold then grows branches into the worm and derives nourishment from it.

We need not look only to the plant and animal kingdom and to the skies to see the wonderful works of God. Our own bodies are "fearfully and wonderfully made" (Ps. 139:14).

"Great and marvellous are thy works, Lord God Almighty; just and true are thy ways, thou King of saints" (Rev. 15:3).

2. The Conflict between Science and the Bible

When we think of a conflict between science and the Bible we tend to think first about the evolution problem. But there is a more basic issue. The basic conflict between science and the Bible arises because of the nature of the scientific method itself. There is no need for conflict here, but the fact remains that there is.

The basis of the scientific method is the assumption that under the same circumstances the same cause will always produce the same effect. Generally this is true, and for untold numbers of generations before the age of science, people employed this principle in the process of learning from experience. The change which the age of science brought about was that investigations were carried out in the form of experiments and that the principle of the uniformity of nature came to be accepted as true in all circumstances. It did, indeed, hold true in many more circumstances than previously had been supposed. As a result many superstitions were shown to be false through a scientific understanding of cause and effect relationships. But this brought the scientists to boast repeatedly that, given time, science would explain everything. Thus they relegated all religion to the realm of superstition and denied the possibility of miracles.

Influenced by the findings of the men of science, liberal

religious leaders sought natural explanations for Biblical miracles. It was said that when the Lord walked upon the water, He merely was walking upon a submerged sandbar. When the multitudes were fed with a few loaves and fishes, it was alleged that what really happened was that the people were shamed into bringing out victuals they had brought along but had concealed until this time because they did not wish to share. Lepers who were cleansed miraculously of their leprosy were said to have been merely dirty and not leprous at all. The raising of Lazarus, four days dead in the tomb, was too difficult to explain, and so it was said to be just a made-up story. Such "explanations" denied the divine inspiration of the Bible and made liars of those who were eye-witnesses to these things. It often turned out that the "explanations" were quite fantastic when examined in detail.

The public has been influenced through the accomplishments of science to believe that every phenomenon must have a natural explanation. In the end this denies not only the supernatural acts of God but also the value of intercessory prayer, and finally the very existence of God.

The assumption that every phenomenon has a natural explanation is itself based upon faith, and those who propagandize the view that science holds all the answers for mankind are themselves evangelizing an anti-Christian religion. Some who do this show such zeal it appears that they are not motivated by an interest in science but by a diabolical desire to oppose the works of God, and especially by a desire to discredit the atonement of Christ.

The scientific method is a means of accomplishment, and it is effective because miracles are not expected in the laboratory. But God is sovereign and He can perform miracles when it suits His purpose. The world was created through a series of miracles, and the virgin birth of Christ — acceptance of which is fundamental to the Christian faith — was a miracle.

3. A Transit of Venus

The great astronomer John Kepler had predicted mathematically that on December 6, 1631, the planet Venus would pass in front of the sun. Kepler himself did not live to see this day, but a Frenchman named Pierre Gassendi, prepared to observe the phenomenon. He watched in vain, for Venus made its transit across the face of the sun after the sun had set in Europe.

According to Kepler, a transit would not occur again for over a hundred years. But an English boy in his teens, Jeremiah Horrocks, did some figuring of his own and found that Venus should repeat its performance in just a few years. Going over his calculations, he found that indeed it was so and that Venus again should pass in front of the sun on December 4, 1639. He was too timid to mention this to anyone except his best friend, William Crabtree.

Modern astronomers can tell at what time of day such a phenomenon will be visible at any place on earth where it can be seen, but the calculations of Jeremiah Horrocks told him only the day, and it was to be a Sunday. If he saw this transit he would be the first to do so, for no one ever before had observed Venus move across the disk of the sun. After this day no one on earth would have an opportunity to see it for a hundred twenty-one years. Besides the rarity of the event it had important theoretical implications in the science of astronomy.

But the transit was due to occur on a Sunday and "the inward voice seemed to tell him that the Creator Himself is more worthy of worship than the phenomena He has instituted for admiration." He watched the sun without interruption from sunrise until it was time to go to church. He went to church. When he returned he hastened to his telescope. The transit had just begun! Where his friend Crabtree was watching, the sky was cloudy but it cleared long enough for him to see it also and to confirm the observation of Horrocks.

It is interesting to note, in contrast to this, the experience of a Frenchman named Legentil who went to India to observe the next transit of Venus a hundred twenty-one years later. Because a war was in progress his ship was delayed and he did not reach land until after the transit was over. As the following transit was to occur only eight years later, he decided to remain in India and wait. When the day of the transit arrived the sky was cloudy and he saw nothing of it. After being shipwrecked twice on his way home, he arrived in France to find his heirs preparing to divide his possessions.

Between that time and the present, Venus has crossed the face of the sun twice. The next transit will occur on June 8, 2004.

It is indeed remarkable that a boy in his teens could make a calculation of greater exactitude than the great Kepler. It also is remarkable that he would risk missing such an event instead of missing church one Sunday.

4. Stones from the Sky

For centuries it was believed that stone axeheads and other stone implements made by uncivilized people were thunderbolts and that they had fallen from the sky. In support of this belief people reported finding the weapons at the exact place where lightning had been observed to strike. Because of another false belief — that lightning does not strike twice at the same place — stone implements were placed in the walls of houses in France and Scandinavia as recently as the last century. Besides being based upon several faulty observations, this implies that lightning can be deceived so that it will not strike where there is circumstantial evidence that it has struck previously.

In 1649 Andrianus Tollius explained how stone axeheads are formed. He did not offer this as a theory but stated it as though an established fact. He said: "They are generated in the sky by the circumflex humor and as it were baked by intense heat; and the weapon becomes pointed by the damp mixed with it flying from the dry part, leaving the other denser; but the exhalations press it so hard that it breaks through the cloud and makes thunder and lightning."

However, stones and chunks of metal really do fall from the sky. Generally such matter burns up due to friction as it falls through the earth's atmosphere, but many pieces reach the earth and are known as meteorites. Strangely, it was be-

14

lieved just as strongly by the erudite that meteorites could *not* have fallen from the sky as it was believed that human artifacts *did* fall from the sky. It seems that until a shower of small meteorites occurred in France in 1803 and forced a change of opinion, scientists in general and astronomers in particular did not believe stones could fall from the sky. They said it was impossible and that therefore it was not true. They contended that those who claimed to have observed meteorites fall were liars, or that the observations were faulty.

While scientists held the erroneous belief that stones could not fall from the sky, others came to the equally incorrect conclusion that stones which fell from the sky must be sacred. There are numerous examples of meteorites which have been revered as sacred in Asia, Europe, and even in America. The black stone in the "holiest of holies" of the Mohammedans is no doubt a meteorite. An object which fell down from the sky (the word *image* does not occur in the original) was revered in the city of Ephesus (Acts 19:35).

There is a Stone which came down from above which is a Stone to be revered and worshipped. This is "the Stone which the builders rejected" and which has become "the head of the corner" (Matt. 21:42). This is the Lord Jesus Christ. In the Bible the Lord is referred to at least seventeen times as a stone or rock. As He came down from above, He also ascended again (Acts 1:9-11; John 14:2, 3, etc.).

With the present emphasis on the scientific method, which has brought about a denial of the supernatural, many are saying that what the Bible says about Christ could not happen and therefore it is not true. They deny that the Lord came from above and profess that He was a man as other men. To those who would not believe when He was on earth He said, "You are from below, I am from above; you are of this world; I am not of this world . . . you shall die in your sins; for unless you believe that I am he, you shall die in your sins" (John 8:23, 24).

On the same occasion He said to those who believed, "If you abide in my word, then you are truly disciples of mine; and you shall know the truth, and the truth shall make you free" (John 8:31, 32).

5. The Rainbow

As sunlight strikes drops of rain it produces the familiar arch of colors called the rainbow. For a long time men have wondered about the rainbow and have tried to explain it. The first time mathematics was applied to a scientific problem, aside from the fields of astronomy, optics, and music was Aristotle's solution to the problem of how the rainbow is formed. His method was ingenious, though some of his assumptions were incorrect, and the result was incorrect by modern standards. Although there was great interest in the rainbow, this work of Aristotle was not surpassed for nearly two thousand years.

Explanations of the phenomenon of the rainbow were proposed by many men, including the great astronomer John Kepler. It is strange that so brilliant a man as Kepler contended for some time that the rainbow was produced by the spherical shape of clouds (instead of the spherical shape of raindrops) when it is so obvious that clouds are not spherical in shape.

In the first part of the seventeenth century Rene Descartes believed he had solved the problem of the rainbow through the use of geometry and trigonometry. In the latter half of that century Isaac Newton invented the calculus, and he and others applied it to the problem. As time went on it became evident that even calculus is not an adequate tool to solve the problem of the rainbow and that still more advanced mathematical techniques must be employed. Although it appears that modern methods have just about solved the problem, some questions still may remain to be answered.

The Bible says that after the flood at the time of Noah the Lord gave the rainbow as the token of the covenant which He made with all living creatures that there never again would be a universal flood. Since the rainbow is a physical phenomenon, apparently resulting from principles which existed from the beginning, some commentators try to avoid the implication that the rainbow was first seen after the flood, and they say that at that time the Lord chose the rainbow for a symbol of His covenant. The Bible says that before the flood the earth was watered by a mist rather than by rain. Also there is some evidence that the earth at that time was surrounded by a vapor canopy which collapsed when "the windows of heaven were opened" (Gen. 7:11) at the time of the flood. Under these conditions it may very well be that no rainbow was seen before the flood.

Rainbows are not all alike, for at different times different colors may predominate. It has been found that this is due to differences in the size of the raindrops. This predominance of different colors at different times has led to a superstition that has persisted to modern times, that it can be told which crops will produce the highest yield by noticing which colors predominate in rainbows observed during the growing season.

In ancient Icelandic and Scandinavian literature the rainbow, or the goddess represented by the rainbow, is presented as a link between the gods and man. But the Bible says that the Lord Jesus Christ is the only mediator between God and man.

During medieval times there was a tradition that there would be no rainbow for forty years before the end of the age. Because of this tradition people had a sense of comfort and false security when they saw a rainbow, for they believed they were safe for at least another forty years. This is quite contrary to Scripture in two particulars. The Bible tells us that the return of Christ is imminent and has been so ever since He ascended into heaven from the Mount of Olives in the sight of His disciples. The Lord could come at any time. Furthermore, for Christians, the return of the Lord and the consummation of the age are not to be dreaded, but are a time to be anticipated with joy, "looking for that blessed hope and the glorious appearing of the great God and our Savior Jesus Christ" (Titus 2:13).

6. Leaven

In the Bible yeast is called *leaven*. Leaven decomposes dough to a condition where it ferments and produces alcohol and carbon dioxide. The dough becomes acidic and is called sour. It is believed that in this way we got our word *sour* from the Hebrew word for leaven, which is *seor*.

Leaven was forbidden in any sacrifice to the Lord which was placed upon the altar. (It was permitted in sacrifices eaten by the priests and not placed upon the altar.) The reason that leaven was not permitted in offerings to the Lord was because of the quality which it possesses to decompose materials. An attribute of the Lord is His unchanging and eternal being. Something which has qualities of decomposition and corruption is not suitable to be included in offerings to Him.

Leaven was particularly forbidden in the Passover meal. The Passover also was called the feast of unleavened bread. In the Passover there is much symbolism related to the atoning death of Christ. At the last supper, which occurred at the time of Passover, the Lord Jesus Christ said of the bread, "This is my body." His body did not experience corruption in the tomb. The instructions were very explicit that the bread which represented His body should have no leaven in it.

On the other hand, offerings to the Lord could be seasoned with salt. In contrast to the symbolism of corruption represented by leaven, salt tends to prevent corruption and it represents a purifying and preserving influence. The Lord said to His disciples, "Ye are the salt of the earth."

Some years ago a prominent Communist commented favorably on the growing trend in which nominal Christians and Communists approach each other to seek common ground in which each may find something beneficial in the other. He said that while Karl Marx called religion the opium of the people, it now is becoming the yeast of the people. This change in symbolism will sound hopeful to some, but in the Bible leaven symbolizes the spread of evil doctrine.

The Lord warned His disciples to beware of the leaven of the Pharisees and Sadducees (Matt. 16:6-12). We need to beware of the corrupting influence of infiltrating false doctrines.

7. The Sponge

There are some three thousand species of sponges. Most people would not recognize even the commercial sponge as a sponge if they saw it in its natural condition. Sponges have a structure which is unlike that of any other living creature. It was only about three hundred years ago that it was recognized that even the familiar commercial sponge is an animal. The sponge is mentioned only once in the Bible.

Shortly before our Lord was nailed to the cross He was offered "vinegar" (sour wine) mixed with "gall" (Matthew) or "myrrh" (Mark.). It is believed that this mixture had properties of a mild anesthetic and was customarily offered to the condemned to ease their pain. When the Lord tasted it and found it to be such a mixture, He refused it. Thus He suffered the full extent in making the sacrifice that redeems us.

While on the cross He said, "I thirst," and was given wine in a sponge. Matthew and Mark say that in order to elevate the sponge it was placed upon a reed. John does not mention the reed but says that they "put *it* upon hyssop." The word "it" is in italics, showing that it does not appear in the original text. The original can be translated to mean "a sponge with hyssop" instead of "a sponge upon hyssop."

It commonly is assumed that the hyssop mentioned by John is the same as the reed mentioned by Matthew and Mark, but hyssop is a bushy plant of the mint family and is not at all like a reed. It would be quite unsuitable to use hyssop as a means of raising the sponge of wine to the Lord upon the cross.

In those days hyssop was widely used as a condiment and when added to food or drink it produced a cooling effect. Apparently the wine had some hyssop mixed with it. It was soaked in a sponge and attached to the end of a reed.

John tells us that this was done that Scripture might be fulfilled, or in other words, to fulfill prophecy. This is recorded in Psalm 69:21. Psalm 22 is a detailed prophecy of the crucifixion and it begins, "My God, my God, why hast Thou forsaken me?" These words were uttered by the Lord upon the cross. God the Father had to forsake Him at that time while He bore our sins. As a result, we never are forsaken.

8. Flies That Look Like Bees

The drone fly, *Eristalis tenax,* looks so much like a honey bee that it commonly is mistaken for one. Moreover, it frequents flowers and feeds on nectar and pollen. The great French naturalist Reaumur remarked that he scarcely ever dared to take one in his hand without hesitating, although he knew it was a harmless fly.

But in keeping with its true identity as a fly, the drone fly lays its eggs in putrifying matter, such as the carcass of an animal. Among the people of ancient Greece, Rome, and other nations, and through the middle ages, there was a widespread belief that the decaying flesh of cattle produced bees. It seems nearly certain that they got this idea because they observed drone flies circling over carion, and they saw the next generation of flies emerge.

There were various recipes for obtaining quality bees from dead flesh. For example, one advocated by an African king named Juba, who lived at the time of Christ, gave specific directions. The ox used must be thirty months old, it must be fat, and it must be killed by being beaten with clubs without shedding any blood. Certain herbs were to be strewn over the body. It was to be sealed for three weeks in a building of specified size and shape. The building then was to be ventilated and the bees would appear eleven days later. It seems amazing that such beliefs could continue so long, for no one ever got a drop of honey in this way.

But this belief was held not only in ancient and medieval

times nor was it accepted only by the ignorant, for it persisted among scholars into the seventeenth century. The great Italian naturalist Aldrovanali (1602), the English naturalist Moufet (1634), and the French scholar Bochart (1663) all accepted it as a fact.

Clutus, a botanist of Leyden, published a book about bees in 1597 in which he pointed out the error of mistaking flies for bees. In 1738 Reaumur attributed the belief that bees came from dead cattle to have originated because flies resembling bees were mistaken for bees. He did not refer to *Eristalis tenax* by name because at that time it had not yet been given its modern scientific name. Pointing out the fly by its scientific name was first done by the Baron C. R. Osten Sacken, a Russian diplomat.

Wherever this strange belief is mentioned, one is likely to see a reference to Samson and the bees he found in the carcass of a lion he previously had slain. It usually is stated that this demonstrates an ancient origin for the belief that bees developed from decaying flesh, implying that Samson saw flies and mistook them for bees. When the Baron Sacken wrote that *Eristalis* no doubt was the insect responsible for this ancient error, he sent a copy of his paper to the German professor of Scriptural exegesis Adelbert Merx. Professor Merx then produced a "learned paper" in which he expressed his acceptance of *Eristalis tenax* as Samson's bees. But the baron and the professor both overlooked the fact that Samson found honey inside the carcass, and flies do not make honey. So Samson did not see *Eristalis tenax* after all. He ate of the honey and gavè some of it to his parents and they also ate. It follows that the carcass of the lion must have been cleaned out by scavengers and what was left of it mummified. Bees would not use a decaying carcass for a hive, and even if they did there would be no place to fasten the honeycombs. Moreover, a human being of a civilized society would not wish to eat anything coming from carion swarming with flies.

When people thought that dead cattle could become transformed into living bees it was natural that bees should become a symbol of the resurrection and immortality. It is known that initiates into the ancient religion of Mithraism wore figures of bees on their garments to signify rebirth and immortality. Most Christians probably never have heard of Mithraism, although at one time it was the chief rival of Christianity and its influence is still with us. The most important of the many festivals of Mithras was his birthday, celebrated on December 25. Mithras generally was considered to be the sun or daylight, and hence his birthday was at the time of the winter solstice, when the days begin to get longer. This later was fixed as the birthday of Christ in an effort to make it easier for the pagans to switch from worshipping Mithras to worshipping Christ, which was a mistake and did not work. It merely brought pagan practices into Christian worship.

The acceptance of the bee as a symbol of immortality was based upon a deception. The "bee" really was a fly, and there was no resurrection involved — the animals from which the flies came really were dead and remained that way. A name for Satan is Beelzebub, which means "Lord of Flies." Satan is the author of deception, and through false religious movements he presents various false hopes of immortality.

In the most frequently cited formula for producing bees from cattle, one of the specifications is that the animal must be beaten to death with clubs without shedding any blood. It is difficult if indeed possible at all to kill an ox with clubs without shedding blood. This again is indicative of a false hope of immortality based upon an impossible method of achieving it. All of Satan's methods of achieving eternal life are bloodless or are based upon animal blood, which cannot cleanse from sin. It is only the shed blood of Christ in atonement that can make the sinner clean.

9 Automation among the Bees

The first mention of honey in the Bible is in Genesis, where Jacob sent some honey with other gifts to the man in Egypt who turned out to be Joseph.

The keeping of bees to produce more honey than the bees require for themselves has been practiced from antiquity but the modern improvements in the means of obtaining honey and pollinating crops have been accomplished through the accommodation of men to the ways of bees and not vice versa.

As early as 1788 M. J. E. Spitzner suggested that bees which find a new source of food are able to communicate its location to other bees by a system of gyrations and vibrations. Somewhat over a century and a half later, about 1946, Karl von Frisch cracked the bees' code and discovered how they transmit to others the direction and distance from the home position to the new source of nectar.

In 1959 Wolfgang Steche made a mechanical bee which can be maneuvered electronically by remote control. This electronic bee can be made to girate and vibrate so as to signal to the bees any direction and distance the operator desires.

Lorus J. Milne suggests that the present knowledge of means to direct bees to any location by means of an electronic bee enables us to replace the scout bees with automation. He proposes that a human observer in a light airplane communicate by radio the location of areas ready for pollination to a man on the ground who then transmits the information by means of a mechanical bee to bees which have been brought near the site in a mobile unit.

The ability of worker bees to measure distances, to compute the angle between a line from the hive to the destination and a line from the hive to the sun (even when going around obstacles) and to transmit these facts to other workers in the hive is innate in the bees and does not have to be learned. Besides this amazing behavior pattern, the workers have marvellous physical adaptations for the work they do. This is all the more remarkable because the workers do not reproduce themselves but are the progeny of the queens and drones, which do not have these endowments and have no use for them. Charles Darwin found himself in a very difficult position when he attempted to explain the evolution of social insects by his theory of survival of the fittest. If some bees became genetically better adapted for their work, they would perish without passing it on to their offspring, for they have none.

During the winter months honeybees form a mass and produce heat by muscular exertion. The colder the temperature in the environment, the more heat they produce — up to a temperature of 94° Fahrenheit. At this critical temperature the queen starts to lay eggs. Laying eggs at this time of the year is not in the best interest of the bees and may destroy the colony.

If the bees gained their wonderful adaptations through a process of Darwinian natural selection or survival of the fittest over a long period of time, it does not seem reasonable that they would have a defective behavior of this sort. If they gained anatomical and behavioral adaptations which are so complex as to be quite amazing, why would they not have eliminated a defective trait which is much simpler? They could cease their temperature-raising activity before the critical 94° is reached or queens could refrain from laying eggs at this temperature. Either or both of these would be much more easily accomplished through survival of the fittest than the bringing about of other adaptations which they have.

Even though our knowledge has increased to where bees can be replaced by automation, there is still much that is not understood if a naturalistic explanation is sought.

10. The Fish

The early Christian church used the fish very widely as a symbol. Because of persecution Christians found it advisable to have a secret way of recognizing each other. This was accomplished by drawing an outline of a fish. It is believed that the fish was selected as a suitable symbol because the letters of the Greek word for fish are the initials for: *Jesus Christ, Son of God, Savior.*

The Bible has been under attack for a long time and aspersions have been cast upon everything that is truly Christian, so it is not surprising that some have suggested that the Christians chose the fish because various non-Christian people in those days considered fish to be sacred. This is ridiculous. The Christian faith is the fulfillment of Judaism, most of the early Christians were Jews, and the Jews at this time were strict monotheists. To Christians in those days, as today, the Old Testament is the inspired Word of God, and it condemns polytheism and idolatry. Idolatrous objects were strictly forbidden, and fish were specifically mentioned in Deuteronomy 4:18.

It is true that fish had a part in the religious life of the nations around Palestine. In Egypt the eel was considered sacred. To the Syrians all fish were sacred, and for that reason not to be eaten. The chief god of the Philistines was Dagon. In spite of the opposing belief of some scholars, it seems that Dagon was a fish-god. The feminine counterpart of Dagon was Atargatis, who was represented as part woman and part fish.

In the city of Ascalon in what is now Israel there was a temple of Atargatis with a pool of sacred fish. The fish were fed every day and were eaten only by the priests of the goddess. At Hierapolis in Asia Minor there was another such temple, and the fish in its pool were adorned with golden ornaments.

In I Samuel 5 it is recorded that the Philistines took the ark of God, after they had captured it from the Israelites, and brought it to the temple of their god Dagon. The next day they were surprised to find that the image of Dagon had fallen on its face before the ark of God. The idolatrous Philistines set Dagon up again in his place, and the following morning they found him fallen again before the ark of God. This time in falling, the idol had broken. "And the head of Dagon and both the palms of his hands *were* cut off upon the threshold: only *the stump of* Dagon was left him." The words in italics were not in the original text and have been supplied by the translators. Linguists say that the word *Dagon* refers to a fish, with an endearing suffix. In other words, the original text, without the words in italics, says that the head and hands were broken off and only the fishy part was left. In pictures Dagon was represented as having the head and hands of a man, and sometimes also feet, together with the body of a fish.

People who held fish as sacred refrained from eating them, or their priests alone partook of them, apparently as a symbolic means of drawing closer to the deity to whom the fish were sacred. This, of course, was not true of the early Christians. Some of the Lord's disciples were fishermen. They earned their living catching fish and they had no scruples about eating them. On two separate occasions the Lord multiplied a few prepared fish into many to feed a multitude. In recruiting disciples the Lord told them that they would become "fishers of men," and they left their fishing to learn how to win men for the Lord.

11. Serpents in the Wilderness

In John 3:14, 15, just before the most well-known verse of the Bible, the Lord Jesus Christ said to Nicodemus, "And as Moses lifted up the serpent in the wilderness, even so must the Son of man be lifted up, that whosoever believeth in Him should not perish but have eternal life."

The reference to the serpent being lifted up in the wilderness alludes to the incident of Numbers 21:4-9, where the Lord sent fiery serpents among the people because of their continued complaining. People who were bitten by the serpents died. When the others repented, the Lord told Moses to make an image of a serpent in brass and to raise it upon a pole. Whoever was bitten and looked upon the brazen serpent would live. This, of course, was a miraculous provision for saving their lives. The Lord told Nicodemus that as the brazen serpent was raised, He also would be raised in crucifixion, and that those who looked to Him with faith would live.

As scientists attempt to explain all miracles on a natural basis, the miracle of the brazen serpent in the wilderness has not escaped their attention. Various textbooks and encyclopedias say that the fiery serpents were guinea worms. The guinea worm is not a serpent at all. It is a parasitic worm which is contracted by ingesting the egg in drinking water. The adult female is two to four feet long and only a twenty-fifth of an inch in diameter. It lives just beneath the surface of the skin and produces an ulcer, through which it lays its eggs. Such a creature is an unlikely candidate for the fiery serpents encountered by the Israelites in the wilderness, but the scientists have chosen them for this office. A brazen image of such a worm would merely be about four feet of wire, hardly an image to inspire idolatry — but later (II Kings 18:4) the image of the serpent which Moses had made had to be destroyed because the people were burning incense to it.

To remove a guinea worm people take hold of it at the ulcer it causes and wrap it around a stick. They take several turns a day until the entire length has been removed. If the worm is broken during this procedure it can cause death to the person. Some books actually state that this method of removing the "fiery serpents" was originated by Moses! What a travesty upon the words of Scripture!

12. Swans

Swans are among the most graceful and beautiful of birds. Not only are they beautiful and graceful but also they are models of marital fidelity. They mate for life and the parents share in the responsibilities of raising the young. But there is another side to the swan's nature which most people do not suspect, for without provocation a swan can become suddenly savage and cunningly cruel.

A small boy was feeding cake to some swans when suddenly one of them pulled him into the stream and toward the deep water while the others pecked at him. He nearly was drowned before he was rescued. Another young boy was playing in shallow water while his attendant sat on the bank nearby. Three swans appeared around a bend in the river and surrounded the boy. One of them pulled him into deep water while the other two kept the adult attendant away. Before help could be summoned the child was drowned.

It is not always small children that are attacked by swans. A ten year old girl was pulled into the water and drowned by a single swan. Another swan attacked an adult riding a bicycle, breaking his nose and blinding him permanently in one eye.

Swans illustrate for us something of the nature of Satan, for when it suits his purpose he can appear as an angel of light, though his intention is to destroy man. Just what the swan's "motive" is we can only surmise, but we know that

Satan aspired to be like God, and failing, became the enemy of God. Since God's plan for man is salvation from the penalty of sin through the sacrificial death of Christ upon the cross, the purpose of Satan became the prevention of man's obtaining this free gift of salvation.

Paul tells us that Satan can make himself appear as an angel of light, and so it is not surprising that his ministers can appear as ministers of righteousness. Many who would shun anything that resembled evil are attracted by the platitudes of a false gospel. Paul says, and repeats for emphasis, that even though an angel from heaven preach any other gospel than salvation through the atoning death of Christ, let him be accursed (Gal. 1:8, 9).

The lure of a pretty appearance may entice the unwary to destruction. In the spiritual world, as in the natural world, safety comes through knowing the nature of the enemy. There is a simple test which reveals whether a teaching is of God or of the devil, and this is the blood test — unless it exalts the blood of Christ, shed for the remission of sins, it is not of God.

13. Birds of Paradise

The birds of paradise probably are the most beautiful birds in the world. The natural habitat of most of them is in remote areas of New Guinea, and for a long time the only knowledge Europeans had of them was from skins sold to traders by natives. In preparing these skins the natives removed the legs and feet. This gave rise to a belief, accepted even by the erudite, that the birds remained constantly in the air, never alighting, and that specimens were obtained only when they died and fell to the earth. It was said that they always faced the sun and that they lived so high in the air that they were not visible from the ground. It was believed that the female laid its eggs in a hollow on the back of the male and brooded them while the male remained in perpetual flight. It was thought that they subsisted entirely upon "the dew of heaven," and some maintained that they had no internal organs but merely masses of fat in the area occupied by the viscera of ordinary birds.

In the seventeenth century a naturalist named John Johnstone published a work on natural history which went through several editions and was translated into a number of languages. In it he confirmed the footlessness of these birds and gave the notion wide publicity. In 1758 the great Linnaeus gave the best-known species the scientific name *Paradisaea apoda,* which means "the footless bird of paradise." It carries this technical name to this day.

We may marvel that because of a misunderstanding about the way the natives prepared skins, intelligent people could have believed such fantastic things about the birds of paradise. But today in some of the anti-Christian cults intelligent people are believing things which are quite fantastic also.

Modern evolutionary ornithologists believe that the birds of paradise are closely related to the crows. This may be verified by consulting practically any book or scientific journal which deals with this subject. For example, the *Encyclopedia Britannica* says they are "closely related to the bowerbird and crow." Ernst Mayr, a noted scientist who is a specialist in the classification of birds and who made a special study of the birds of paradise while curator of the world's finest collection of these birds, says, "Birds of paradise are believed to be resplendent relatives of the crow family." He also refers to "their relatives, the crows."

One of the students of Thomas Henry Huxley, named W. K. Parker, went so far as to say that from a study of their anatomy he would "place the birds of paradise in a position almost exactly intermediate between the true Crow of the Old World and the Piping Crow of Australia."

An Australian scientist named Tom Iredale published a book about birds of paradise in 1950. According to him the belief that these birds are closely related to crows is not scientific at all, but is the outgrowth of a misunderstanding. He says that about two hundred years ago someone was trying to describe the size of the greater bird of paradise and said it was about the size of a crow. Over a hundred years ago Alfred Russell Wallace, co-author with Charles Darwin of the natural selection theory of evolution, also compared the greater bird of paradise with a crow as to size. Mr. Iredale believes that it is merely because of these references to the crow in comparing the birds as to size that the notion got started that they are related. He strongly disagrees with the opinion that crows and birds of paradise are related and says that "it must be emphasized that no bird of paradise shows any, even distant, relationship with any crow."

This is another instance of what appears to be a general rule: No matter what belief is held by evolutionists about some detail of the theory, it is always possible to find at least one evolutionist who holds the opposite view.

14. Cowbirds and Cuckoos

Cowbirds never build a nest. They lay their eggs in the nests of other birds. The egg of the cowbird usually hatches before the other eggs in the nest and the young cowbird grows more rapidly than the other nestlings. The young cowbird calls for more attention, and gets it, than do the others. The rightful inhabitants of the nest may die as a result.

Alexander Wilson, called "the father of American ornithology," at one time took a tolerant attitude toward cowbirds, but as he learned to know them better he changed his mind. He described the female as "lacking every moral and maternal instinct." Cowbirds do not pair but are promiscuous and "the male offers the same amenities to any female, indiscriminatingly, and they are reciprocated accordingly, without exciting either restraint or jealousy in any of the party."

People who have made a study of cowbirds say that in many cases their dupes appear to be completely unaware of the fact that they are harboring and nourishing an enemy. Unless the birds notice the intrusion immediately and do something about it right away, they never rid themselves of the usurper. In fact, they still may be feeding the demanding cowbird when it is twice as large as themselves and quite able to take care of itself.

When birds notice the strange egg of the cowbird in their nest they act as though very much upset, but in the end most of them do nothing effective about it. As a result they raise a cowbird, to the detriment of their own species.

Yellow warblers, on the other hand, frequently do something about it. They construct another nest above the first to avoid incubating the cowbird egg. If the cowbird lays another egg in the new nest, the yellow warblers build still another nest on top of the others. A number of observers have reported finding yellow warbler nests four stories high, with cowbird eggs in the abandoned lower levels. This is more work for the warblers and they even have to abandon some of their own eggs in the process, but they seem to value their independence and freedom sufficiently to do this.

Cowbirds lay speckled eggs and they prefer to put them in the nests of other species which also have speckled eggs. Thus the difference is not so obvious and infiltration may be accomplished with greater ease. Various observers say that when the cowbird lays an egg in the nest of a robin, which has light blue unspeckled eggs, the robin usually throws out the egg immediately, accompanied with a sound which one is tempted to compare to a human exclamation of disgust.

As it is difficult for the cowbird to infiltrate the robins because of the striking difference in the eggs, so enemies of the Christian faith cannot infiltrate so easily where people are strict Bible-believers and conduct their affairs along Scriptural lines. Where the difference between church members and enemies of the faith is not clear, infiltration is easy.

Another parasitic bird is the European cuckoo. Like the cowbird, the cockoo lays its eggs in the nests of other birds. Before the young cuckoo develops feathers and before its eyes are open it systemmatically empties the nest of its foster family. It works its body under a rightful nestling and then, raising itself upon its powerful legs, it heaves the other nestling over the edge of the nest. With its large unfeathered wings it feels around to make sure the job of ousting the rightful inhabitants of the nest has been accomplished with completeness. If the cuckoo could speak it no doubt would call anyone "bigoted" who challenged its right to do this.

Cuckoos lay eggs of different colors and in order to deceive will even seek out nests with eggs of the same color as those to be deposited. To the foster parents these eggs may seem similar but the birds that hatch from them are fundamentally different. They may "compromise" to the extent of having similar egg shells, but the nature of the bird will not change.

Some men, as well as some birds, just will not learn by experience.

15. The Unicorn

The seventy scholars who translated the Old Testament into Greek in the third century B.C. found themselves facing a real problem when they came to the Hebrew word *re'em*. From the text they learned that this was the name of a strong, swift, and intractable beast. Apparently this animal was well known to the Hebrews, but the translators, who were living in Egypt a long time after the writing of the original, did not know which animal was meant.

A Greek historian named Ctesias had brought back a report of the Indian rhinoceros in the fifth century B.C., and apparently the seventy scholars thought that the description best fitted this beast for they translated the Hebrew word as *monokeros*. This means an animal with one horn, and the Indian rhinoceros has one horn. Later the Latin Vulgate translation, which was based largely upon the Greek Septuagint, used the word *unicornis*, meaning with one horn. The English, German, and French Bibles followed, with the word *unicorn* and its equivalents.

By medieval times the unicorn was thought of as a horse-like animal with a horn on its forehead. The horn was reputed to have medicinal qualities, but it was valued chiefly for its alleged ability to counteract all poisons. Rhinoceros horn was not everywhere accepted and sometimes it was called false horn to distinguish it from supposedly true horn of the unicorn. Something was most likely to be accepted as true horn if it came from a far away country and from an un-known source. Thus the tusks of narwhals, of mammoths, and even of walruses were sold at fabulous prices to those who could afford this protection from poisoning. It is said that at the peak of this traffic the horn was sold for ten times its weight in gold. Queen Elizabeth had one valued at more than a third of a million dollars at the present rate of ex-change. To the time of Charles II it was used in England to purify the royal food, and in France it was employed in the same way as late as 1789.

Until rather recently there was considerable speculation about which animal really was meant by the word *re'em*. The answer came when Assyrian texts were found picturing the urus, or wild ox, and called it *rimu*, the Assyrian equiva-lent of the Hebrew word *re'em*.

The wild ox seems to have become extinct in Asia not long before the time of Nebuchadnezzar. When the seventy schol-ars were preparing the Septuagint, it still lived in Europe north of the Alps. Later, when Julius Caesar became ac-quainted with it, he commented on its ferocity and its un-usual strength and swiftness. He also recorded that it was captured in a trap which was a pit dug for the purpose, that its hide was used to make shields, and that its horns were greatly prized as trophies.

A report in A.D. 1555 stated that by this time all the re-maining animals were in Lithuania. According to Willy Ley this herd consisted of about thirty individuals, and by 1602 they had been reduced to four. The species became extinct in 1627.

For a long time it was said that there really must be such an animal as the fabulous unicorn because the Bible says so. As the mythological nature of the medieval unicorn be-came apparent and the Royal Society of London showed by an experiment that the horn had no ability whatever to counteract poisons, the references to the unicorn in Scripture became an embarrassment to Christians and a delight to scoffers. But the original text of the Bible said nothing at all about unicorns, and the whole affair arose because the scholars who prepared the Septuagint rendered the Hebrew word *re'em* as *monokeros*. We now know that this animal was the urus or wild ox, *Bos primigenius*.

One by one the supposed errors and difficulties in the Bible are cleared up. Any which may still remain may well be taken in faith with the knowledge that in the fullness of time all difficulties will disappear.

16. Babylonian Creation Stories

Some generations ago the Christian public was told that the Biblical account of creation was based upon Babylonian and Assyrian legends. It did not seem to occur to the experts who made these assertions that the Babylonians and Assyrians might have based their legends upon stories handed down from early times, with ever increasing departure from the truth, while the Biblical account of creation and of subsequent times recounts the same events but with the benefit of divine inspiration.

In the Biblical account of creation there is one God (expressed in the plural to represent the Trinity), while in the legends of Babylonia and Assyria there are many gods. The exploits of these gods strongly suggest that they were deifications of Nimrod and other men of renown who lived before and after the flood. The Biblical account is simple and dignified, while the legends are fantastic stories involving intrigues, slaughters, and drunkenness among the gods.

Marduk, the Babylonian god of creation, had parents, grandparents, and other ancestors for many generations. There are various references among the clay tablets that recount the legends which seem to equate Marduk with Nimrod, the mighty man of valor who lived after the flood and who defied God.

Marduk fought with a goddess named Tiamat. Fighting with a goddess hardly can be considered a gallant deed or act of valor for a god, but according to legend it was the beginning of creation. Marduk slew the goddess and used half of her body to form the earth and the other half to form the heavens. He formed man from the body of a god named Kingu, whom he slew also.

According to the Babylonian view, the purpose for which man was created was to serve and wait upon the gods while they rested. In appreciation for what Marduk had done for them, the lesser gods built him a temple "made of bricks with its head on high." Rather clearly this is an allusion to the Tower of Babel.

The final episode in the Babylonian story of creation contains a number of titles of Marduk, who is proclaimed by the other gods to be the one true God. These other gods really were other ancient men of renown. Thus began the various pagan religions, with Nimrod under various names representing the chief deity.

Pagan religions are still with us. Some have made the mistake of trying to combine paganism and Christianity, hoping in this way to win the pagans. This is not the Biblical method of winning converts and it does not work. Finally there are the critics who make their devastating proclamations with a display of scholarship, attacking the trustworthiness of the Bible. There is sufficient similarity between the Babylonian legends and the Biblical account of creation that the Babylonian stories may have come from a corrupted tradition of events that did occur, but to say that Moses derived the Biblical description of creation from the Babylonian and Assyrian stories is absurd.

17. Sacred Cow

Why were animals first domesticated? The most obvious answer would be so that they would be a source of food and clothing. But some scientists now say that this is not the case and that domestication was started for religious purposes. Furthermore, they say that very likely cattle were the first animals to be domesticated. The horns of wild cattle resembled the crescent moon in shape, and therefore pagan worshippers considered the bovines to be especially suitable as sacrifices to the moon-goddess.

Concerning the first domesticated animals, we learn from the Bible that Abel kept sheep, not cattle. Apparently, the Hebrew word does refer to sheep as distinct from what we call cattle. Scientists who are not Christians disregard this account, but Christians cannot. Our Lord referred to Abel as a real person, and so did Paul.

In an article about this in a scientific journal, it is admitted that the conclusions reached by the scientists are hypothetical and conjectural. Although Scripture does not give us a great deal of information, there are clues from which we may draw conclusions which are more substantial than the conjectures of the scientists.

Before the birth of Cain and Abel sin had entered into the world through disobedience. Also a prophetic statement had been made about the coming Redeemer (Gen. 3:15). We may not be certain how well Eve understood this prophecy, but when Cain was born into the world as the first child, she made a statement which some interpret to mean that she not only understood, but even had a hope that this child would fulfill the prophecy. It is said that "I have gotten a man from the Lord" (Gen. 4:1) is not a correct translation. "With the help of the Lord," is said to be possible, but it involves an unusual use of a Hebrew word. The literal translation is said to be, "I have gotten a man, even Jehovah." It is easy to see why this rendering would be avoided by translators unless it was quite apparent that Eve was expressing the false hope that this child indeed was the promised Redeemer.

Cain was a tiller of the ground and he brought vegetable matter as a sacrifice to the Lord. Abel brought from his flock. This may seem natural and appropriate, but God respected Abel's offering and not Cain's. Some find evidence in the original language, as well as in Paul's use of the plural, "gifts," in connection with Abel's offering, that Abel also brought the products of plants in addition to sheep from his flock. A bloodless sacrifice expressed thanksgiving, while an animal sacrifice was a confession of sin and an expression of faith in God's provision for atonement. "Without the shedding of blood there is no remission of sin" (Heb. 9:22).

In Genesis 4:7 Cain was told that if he did not do well "sin lieth at the door." But the word here translated *sin* also means a *sin-offering*. If he recognized his need as a sinner, a suitable offering for sin was close at hand and there was no excuse for him to neglect the opportunity of utilizing it.

There no longer is any need for animal sacrifices, for the Redeemer, Jesus Christ, has come and shed His blood in atonement. Those who apply this sacrifice as the atonement for their sins are accepted by God, as was Abel. But today there are many who rebel against this, as Cain did, and refuse to accept the way God has provided. They intend that the good things they accomplish, some perhaps through much personal sacrifice, will make them acceptable to God. But this is like the bloodless sacrifice of Cain. It is like an offering of thankfulness. But our thankfulness is not acceptable to God until we belong to Him, and this is gained through our redemption by the blood of Christ. We first need to be acceptable to God through the righteousness we receive imputed to us through our accepting Christ's sacrifice in our behalf and then we do things which express our thanks to Him.

18. Cain's Wife

"Where did Cain get his wife?"

This question has been asked over a period of many years and for a variety of reasons. The answer really is quite simple. Cain married one of his sisters.

Marriage between brothers and sisters is not practiced in our society and there is a good reason for this. Undesirable hereditary traits tend to be "recessives." This means that in order to be manifest, hereditary factors for these traits must be received from *both* parents. Since closely related persons are more likely to be carrying the same hereditary factors, close marriages tend to bring out undesirable characteristics. But in the beginning, God created everything good. There is no reason to believe that the first parents had undesirable hereditary factors to transmit to their children, and hence brother-sister marriages would not be detrimental.

Undesirable hereditary factors may accumulate in a population as time goes on, for the hereditary factors or genes may change or mutate at any time, and nearly all mutations are less beneficial than the original gene. A large proportion of them are strongly detrimental. The hereditary condition in which it is difficult to stop bleeding, known as hemophilia, has been traced back in the royal families of Europe to Queen Victoria.

If highly desirable traits are found in a family and defects do not occur, intermarriages will concentrate the good traits.

There was considerable intermarriage in the Bach family, and as a result there were more musicians in that family than there would have been if they had married outside the family.

The Darwin family was rather much intermarried. Charles Darwin married his cousin, Emma Wedgewood, whose father made the famous Wedgewood Chinaware. He had some reason for concern about the closeness of intermarriage in his family, and he had a defective child that died young. But also there were persons of outstanding ability among his descendants.

There was much intermarriage among the Roman Caesars and also considerable insanity. The Ptolemies of Egypt were Greeks and they practiced brother-sister marriage. The famous Cleopatra was in this lineage. Apparently she was rather superior in some ways, but there were others in the family about whose deeds the general public graciously has been spared knowledge.

Abraham married his half-sister Sarah. Isaac married Rebekah, a daughter of Abraham's cousin. Their son, Jacob, married Leah and Rachel, his cousins. From these close marriages came the Hebrew people. They were strong and vigorous and favored by the Lord. Many promises were made to them by God. Some of these promises have been fulfilled and some remain to be fulfilled in the future. The most wonderful of these will occur when they recognize and accept their Messiah.

The Bible says that Adam was created as an individual and therefore there was no mate for him. To remove any possible grounds for quibbling, Scripture describes how the first woman was produced from a portion of his side. For those who do not accept this — and they are legion today — there is no problem as to where Cain got his wife, for they consider Cain to be a part of a myth. But some of them like to try to embarrass believers by asking them where Cain

got his wife. But there is no problem here for believers because under the circumstances laid down in the Bible, the
wife of Cain could only have been his sister.

Josephus, the great historian of the Jews, wrote about
Adam's children. His writing, of course, was not inspired and
came from tradition. He says that Adam "was solicitous for
posterity and had a vehement desire for children. . . . He
had many other children."

In those days people lived a long time and, no doubt, could
produce many children in a lifetime. The Bible tells us that
after the birth of Seth, Adam lived eight hundred years and
"begat sons and daughters" (Gen. 5:3, 4). God gave them instructions and the ability to "be fruitful and multiply and re-
plenish [correctly translated *fill*] the earth" (Gen. 1:28).

19. The Walls of Jericho

Scientists try to explain everything. To them, no miracle can be accepted as such. In the past, the favorite explanation for the falling of the walls of Jericho was the sonic vibration theory. According to this theory, as the priests blew the trumpets of rams' horns and the people shouted, the sonic vibrations caused the walls of Jericho to fall down. It is now said that this theory has been proved to be false. It is said that if the walls had fallen because of sonic vibrations, they would have fallen in a different manner and the stones now would be lying in a different pattern. Moreover, it also is said that an earthquake would not have thrown down the walls the way they fell. If an earthquake had done it, the rocks now would be lying in a different configuration.

Quite conveniently, this disproof of the sonic vibration theory and the earthquake theory was not discovered until a new theory was ready to take their place. According to the new theory, Joshua sent men to undermine the walls. The marching of the Israelites around the city of Jericho each day was done in order to distract the people inside the city so that they would not notice the men digging under the walls. After six days of this secret digging the job was completed and the walls were ready to fall. It is not clear why the Israelites walked around the city seven times on the seventh day when once a day for six days gave the workmen sufficient time to complete their digging.

In the end, the proponents of the new theory depend upon the sonic vibrations of the horns and the shouting and the vibrations from the stamping of the Israelites' feet to start the undermined walls to falling.

We know that Rahab's house was built upon the wall. So there probably were other houses on the wall also. The people of Jericho watched the marching Israelites from the wall, the city being closed. With all this activity upon the wall it would have been impossible for the diggers to undermine it and leave it in such a delicate state of balance that it would have been toppled by the sounds of the horns, shouts, and the stamping of feet. It would be a remarkable feat for engineers to carry out such delicate digging under a massive wall with no one else around, but with people running around on top of it, it is absurd.

The basis for the new theory of the falling of the walls is a recent discovery about the nature of the land upon which the city was built. About five feet below the surface is a layer of sandstone. This served as the foundation for the walls and buildings. But this layer of sandstone is only five feet thick. Below it is fifty feet of sand and then another layer of sandstone. The upper layer of sandstone is not strong enough to support a large modern building, and until engineers investigated the sinking of a modern building it was not suspected that the rocky foundation of the city was only five feet thick. However, the modern theorists believe that these facts about the land upon which the city was built "must have been known to Joshua and his remarkable intelligence service." Then "with his knowledge of soil mechanics and enemy mentality" he was able to calculate how to do the job. Incredibly, according to the report, Joshua even knew about the second layer of sandstone sixty feet below the surface of the ground.

The report of the new theory of the fall of the walls ends with these words: "We thought it was a fable. Now we know how it happened and why."

It is remarkable that someone would call the Biblical account a fable and then accept a fabricated story like this.

20. Jacob's Experiment

Jacob had worked a long time for his uncle Laban, tending his flocks. His love for Rachel was so great that he bargained for nothing else, and now that he was ready to return to Canaan he had a family but no resources. Laban did not wish to see him go, for he had prospered greatly through Jacob's management of his flocks, and he proposed that Jacob remain and work for wages.

Jacob suggested that he would remove from the flock all animals of certain specified types and that his wages would be all animals of these types which thereafter were born into the flock. Laban agreed, and to be sure that none would be left with Jacob, he himself separated the specified animals. He then put them into the care of his sons at a considerable distance. Apparently these types were rather rare in the flock, and perhaps he even thought that no more like them would be born to the animals left in Jacob's care.

But Jacob had a plan. He took branches of young trees and peeled off some of the bark. The light colored wood was exposed at places where the bark was removed, and it made a pattern with the darker bark which was left unpeeled. He made patterns resembling the coats of the animals which were to be his, and he placed the rods where the ewes would see them at breeding time. He even went so far as to remove the rods when weaker animals were breeding and replaced them when the stronger animals were present. Before long he had become wealthy, even though Laban did not abide by the original terms of the agreement and kept changing the specifications regarding the patterns which should designate Jacob's animals.

A study of thirty Bible commentaries reveals that most of the authors seem to consider this a natural phenomenon, with the implication that it would work the same way now if repeated by modern herdsmen. A number attribute it to experience gained by Jacob during the previous years of tending his uncle's flocks. A few believe he was instructed by God in a vision to use the rods, while others consider his prosperity due to God's blessing.

Of the thirty commentaries examined, half were published in the nineteenth century, before the scientific world accepted Mendel's discovery of the fundamental laws of heredity. The other half were published during the half century after 1910. In each of these two categories twelve of the fifteen state or imply that Jacob's results were the natural outcome of the method he used. Three in each group attempt to present some evidence that the result is to be expected. One of these was published as late as 1950. It hardly seems necessary to say that this is not correct. Only three of the thirty say that it would not happen this way if repeated now, and contrary to what one might suppose, these three are among the earliest of the commentaries.

The inheritance of spotting and of the various color patterns in these animals is a technical matter which need not be considered here. It is sufficient to say that if the hereditary factors that produce animals of this sort are present in a flock, as they were among Laban's flocks, such animals may appear again in the very first generation after all spotted and patterned animals have been removed. Indeed, with the appropriate crosses the flock could soon become predominantly any pattern desired, which is what happened.

Many miracles are recorded in Scripture but each is done

through divine authority. The rods seem to have been Jacob's idea, and certainly they had nothing to do with what happened. The explanation is given in the next chapter. God saw that Jacob had been unfairly treated by Laban, and He made the appropriate crosses to occur. Jacob was under God's special care, as are all Christians. It is a poor testimony before the world to resort to questionable means to gain a desired end. The end does not justify the means. "Vengeance belongs to me and I will repay, saith the Lord."

21. The Double Revelation Theory

In recent years the "double revelation" view of science and the Scriptures has been espoused and promoted by some Christian men who might not do so if they knew something of its origin and implications.

According to this view, God has given man two revelations. One of these is the revelation through the Bible and the other is a revelation through nature. It is implied or definitely stated that in spiritual and moral matters we should go to the Bible for guidance, but in matters relating to the physical world we should look to nature for the answers.

The eminent Henry Ward Beecher is said to have been the most influential preacher in America for a generation. In New York he built the largest congregation in the nation, starting with nine members. His approach to religion was to liberalize it. In 1885 he published a sermon on "The Two Revelations" and dedicated himself to forwarding the message it contained.

The opening sentence of the sermon was: "That the whole world and the universe were the creation of God is the testimony of the whole Bible . . . but *how* He made them — whether by the direct force of a creative will or indirectly through a long series of gradual changes — the Scriptures do not declare." Beecher was convinced that it was by the latter means over a span of many millions of years. Parallels to this statement of Beecher in his sermon on "the two revelations" may be found today in various articles intended for the guidance of Bible-believing Christians.

Beecher said some things which sound very familiar because we hear them being said today. He told his congregation that evolution is the *method* by which creation came about. He said that evolution no longer is a controversial matter and that 99 per cent of the men of science of his day did not doubt its truth. He enumerated Christian men with well-known names who accepted evolution and found no difficulty in doing so. He praised the evolutionists, calling them "adventurous surveyors who are searching God's handiwork," while those who opposed the views of the evolutionists he called "vaguely bigoted theologists, ignorant pietists, and jealous churchmen." He said that ministers who preached against evolution were "men pretending to be ministers of God [who] with all manner of grimace and shallow ridicule . . . and unproductive wisdom enact the very feats of the monkey in the attempt to prove that the monkey was not their ancestor."

Beecher also spoke of the "grandeur" in the evolutionary concept and assured his people that it would "take nothing away from the grounds of true religion." He preached that a practical result of accepting the evolutionary concept of creation would be the improvement of morality.

Men today have less excuse than Henry Ward Beecher for making such statements. With our advantage of historical perspective we can trace to the evolutionary concept with its "survival of the fittest," together with the philosophy of pragmatism, at least a portion of the blame for such widely diverse evils as juvenile delinquency, unscrupulous practices in big business, the first and second world wars, and the rise of fascism and communism. In the religious sphere it had much to do with the rise to prominence of modernism.

It is frequently said — and it is a corollary of the double revelation theory — that the Bible is not a textbook of science. Since the revelation given by God in Scripture is accepted as a part of the double revelation theory, it follows that those who hold this view should accept as true those parts of the Bible which concern areas in the realm of science. However, the tendency is for these men not to do this. Instead, they put the emphasis on the current views of the scientists, even when these conflict with plain statements of Scripture.

Henry Ward Beecher put much emphasis on the principle of the brotherhood of man. He stressed social action and made slurring remarks about salvation by grace. The espousal of the double revelation theory leads in this direction.

22. Asa Gray and Theistic Evolution

Charles Darwin had three outstanding disciples among the men of science — Thomas Henry Huxley in England, Ernst Haeckel in Germany, and Asa Gray in America. Asa Gray differed from the others in that he professed to be an orthodox Christian. Darwin realized the value of Gray's religious profession in that it tended to make the theory of evolution seem less objectionable to those who opposed it on religious grounds. This influence extends to the present day, and Gray still is presented as an evangelical Christian who saw no incompatibility between his Christian faith and theistic evolution.

Because of the significance attached to Professor Gray's views, it is desirable to inquire just how orthodox he really was. He said of himself, "I dare say I am much more orthodox than Mr. Darwin; also that he is about as far from being an atheist as I am." It seems strange that an evangelical Christian should compare himself with Darwin, who wrote of himself that while he was still a young man he "had come, by this time, to see that the Old Testament . . . was no more to be trusted than the sacred books of the Hindus, or the beliefs of the barbarian." He continued, "Thus disbelief crept over me at a very slow rate, but was at last complete. The rate was so slow that I felt no distress, and have never since doubted even for a single second that my conclusion was correct. I can indeed hardly see how anyone ought to wish Christianity to be true. . . ."

Although Professor Gray never read these words, which Darwin put into the autobiography which he wrote for his children, he knew something of Darwin's religious views, and to the charge that Darwin was an infidel he replied, "Can't say till you tell me what you mean by infidel — and perhaps not then." This does not sound like the language of an evangelical Christian who knows the way of salvation.

Because of Gray's professed orthodoxy Darwin somewhat feared what his reaction would be to *The Descent of Man,* which discussed human evolution. However, Gray responded with a paraphrase of the words of King Agrippa to Paul when Paul declared the gospel to him. Agrippa said, "Almost thou persuadest me to be a Christian." Gray said, "Almost thou persuadest me to have been 'a hairy quadruped with arboreal habits, furnished with a tail and pointed ears.'"

Professor Gray gave his approval to the higher criticism of the Bible, and aspersions cast upon the authority of Scripture by the theory of evolution never bothered him. He seems to have anticipated Neo-Orthodoxy by saying that the Bible contains truth instead of being truth.

One of Darwin's biographers says of Professor Gray, "In America Asa Gray, the great botanist was a convert [to evolution] from the beginning and a most helpful disciple, and his aid was particularly welcome to Darwin, because Gray's eager orthodoxy was helpful in conciliating many whose prejudices would naturally have been averse."

Young people today are accepting evolutionary views because men who have a reputation as conservative Christian men of science are leading them in that direction. The young people defend themselves by saying to parents and friends that it is all right, because these men are evangelical Christians and they say it is all right, so it must be all right. Some of these men really do hold evolutionary views, while others, who would deny that they do, nevertheless say things which lead the young people to believe that they are promoting evolution.

23. Uniformitarianism

In his second Epistle Peter wrote about scoffers in the last days who would reject the promise of the Lord's return, presenting as evidence their observation that "since the fathers fell asleep, all things continue as they were from the beginning of creation." Peter mentions specifically that these people would wilfully disregard the Scriptural account of the flood which destroyed the life which was upon the earth.

The fulfillment of this prophecy may be said to have begun when James Hutton published his *Theory of the Earth* in 1785. He denied the belief held by the scientists of his day that there had been geological events in the past which were of a nature different from those we observe today. He stated that in explaining the origins of geological formations "no powers are to be employed that are not natural to the globe, no action to be admitted except that of which we know the principle." Little attention was taken of his view until 1802, when John Playfair published a book called *Illustrations of the Huttonian Theory*. The prevailing view was that of "catastrophism," which had supernatural connotations, including the Genesis flood.

Charles Lyell, a professional lawyer turned geologist, took up the idea, and he is the one whose writing caused it to become the accepted theory among geologists to the present time. In 1830 he published his three-volume work, *Principles of Geology: Being an Attempt to Explain the Former Changes*

of the Earth's Surface by Reference to Causes Now in Action.
This view is known as uniformitarianism.

The year after the publication of the first volume of Lyell's work, a young man named Charles Darwin set sail on a voyage of scientific exploration which was to last five years. He took with him a copy of the first volume which was given to him by his friend Professor Henslow. The professor told him he would need the book as a naturalist of the expedition because of the facts that it contained, but he cautioned him "on no account to accept the views therein advocated." But this advice was not heeded and the reading of Lyell's book marked the turning point in the life of Charles Darwin.

One biographer says, "Darwin's point of departure from orthodoxy on this voyage was, of course, his reading of the first volume of Lyell's *Principles of Geology*." Another biographer calls it "the book which influenced him more than any other." Still another biographer remarks, "Possibly, without Lyell's *Principles of Geology*, Darwin would not have written his *Origin of Species*." Darwin himself acknowledged his indebtedness to Lyell. He dedicated to Lyell his report of the voyage "as an acknowledgement that the chief part of whatever scientific merit this *Journal* and other works of the author may possess has been derived from studying the well-known and admirable *Principles of Geology*." Years later he said, "I always feel as if my books came half out of Lyell's brain, and that I never acknowledge this sufficiently . . . for I have always thought the great merit of the *Principles* was that it altered the whole tone of one's mind. . . ."

Darwin is the one to whom credit is given for making the theory of evolution acceptable to the men of science, and this theory has had a very prominent place in bringing about the present liberal theology which rejects the gospel of salvation by grace through the atonement of Christ.

But this is not the end of the chain reaction from the pronouncement and acceptance of the uniformitarian principle.

Karl Marx wrote to his colleague Freidrich Engels concerning Darwin's *Origin of Species,* "Darwin's book is very important and serves me as a basis in natural science for the class struggle in history." Marx found Darwin's evolution theory so valuable to his cause that he desired to dedicate his book *Das Kapital* to Darwin, which honor Darwin declined for the reason that he feared it might be displeasing to some members of his family. A boyhood friend of Joseph Stalin tells that when they were in an ecclesiastical school, Stalin read Darwin's book and became an atheist. Others point out that Mussolini and Hitler used Darwinian phrases and catchwords in their speeches.

After more than a century of acceptance of uniformitarianism by the geologists, some recently have begun to doubt that all geological phenomena can be explained in terms of the kinds of changes which are observable today. Norman Newell, paleontologist of the American Museum of Natural History, has said, "Geology suffers from a great lack of data, and in such a situation any attractive theory that comes along is taken as gospel. This is the case with uniformitarianism. . . . But since the end of World War II, when a new generation moved in, we have gotten more data and we have begun to realize that there were many catastrophic events in the past, some of which happened just once."

But as the geologists begin to give up their faith in uniformitarianism and admit that there were geologic effects from "catastrophies" in the past, they will not accept the term "catastrophism." In fact, it is said that this is a "fighting word" with them. The term "catastrophism" has conotations of supernatural acts of God, including the flood at the time of Noah, and this they just will not accept. As Peter said, they willfully disregard the Biblical account of the flood.

24. The Beginning of Life

There is a very important problem about the evolutionary view of the origin of life which is easily overlooked and which is unknown to many people. The evolutionists believe that the earth originally had an atmosphere without an appreciable amount of oxygen and that the oxygen in the atmosphere was produced by the photosynthetic action of green plants. It follows from this that they must assume that life began and existed for some time before there was very much oxygen in the atmosphere.

Even the green plants that give off oxygen in photosynthesis require free oxygen for their own respiration. But there is another dilemma. Scientists at the Southwest Center for Advanced Studies in Dallas, Texas, have shown that before the oxygen in the atmosphere produced a layer of ozone to protect life on earth from deadly rays from the sun, life could not have existed except under about thirty-three feet of water. This depth of water would be required to produce the same amount of screening of lethal rays that is accomplished by the ozone in the atmosphere.

This leads these scientists to admit that life could not have originated in the ocean, as most evolutionists postulate. If life had originated in the ocean, somewhat below the thirty-three foot limit, the churning action of the water would have brought it up into the zone where it would have been killed. Thus they are forced to assert that life must have begun in some quiet inland waters. But even quiet waters have convection currents.

They believe that life may have originated separately at different places on the earth. This leads to the conclusion that unless one form and its descendants destroyed all the others when their ranges eventually overlapped, various forms of life which now seem rather similar may have had a completely different ancestry all the way back to the origin of life.

Also it should be kept in mind that the simplest living cell is "a very advanced evolutionary entity," as these men of science admit. Charles Darwin started with "one or a few" simple forms of life. It is easy to neglect the problem of how the first cell came about. Several evolutionists have stated that from the beginning of organic evolution until the appearance of the first cell is as great an evolutionary span as from the first cell to human beings.

It is characteristic of evolutionary "explanations" that they raise as many problems as they "solve."

25. The Second Law of Thermodynamics

According to the second law of thermodynamics, the universe is like a clock that is running down. The scientists are certain that, unless a creative force is operating, the time will come when the sun and the stars have burned out and the universe will have run down. This running down of the universe is a real problem for the atheists, for how could it have gotten "wound up" in the first place so that now it can be in the process of running down?

Another way of looking at the second law of thermodynamics is that there is a trend toward randomness in the universe. A building will deteriorate and fall apart and its materials become scattered by the forces of nature, but these forces will not assemble a building. There is a trend in nature toward forming less complex distributions of matter from more complex. This is just the opposite of evolution, for according to the theory of evolution, more complex forms have developed from less complex forms. Therefore it has been said that evolution is contrary to the second law of thermodynamics.

Arthur Eddington, the renowned physicist, said that this law holds the supreme position among the laws of nature. He said that if a theory is found to be contrary to the second law of thermodynamics there can be no hope for it. Since the theory of evolution is very much in vogue and the second law of thermodynamics has not been discredited, it follows that the evolutionists must have been able to convince themselves that evolution is not contrary to this law. They get around the difficulty by saying that there is no real difficulty because there is sufficient energy supplied from an outside source, namely the sun.

The second law of thermodynamics can be circumvented *temporarily* by living things in three ways. (1) Human beings are noted for collecting random materials and organizing them — building houses, constructing machines, writing letters and books, and the like. Doing these things requires energy, which comes from food, and can be traced back to the sun. But energy is not enough, for to do these things also requires intelligence and training. (2) A bird can overcome randomness temporarily by collecting scattered materials and building a nest. This also requires energy that can be traced back to the sun as its source, but energy is not enough. An ability which may be called an instinct is necessary. (3) An egg developing into an individual increases in complexity. Energy is required in this transformation, but again energy alone is not enough and there must be in addition a genetic code.

Putting the parts of a watch in a box and shaking them will not assemble the watch, though more energy may be expended in the shaking than would be needed by a watchmaker to do the job. Energy alone is not the answer to the problem of how more complex configurations of matter come about in the world of living things. A genetic code, an instinct, or intelligence is required. The fact that the earth receives energy from the sun is not the answer to the charge that the theory of evolution is contrary to the second law of thermodynamics. Christians are still free to say that this law does contradict the theory of evolution without fear of being called uninformed.

26. Neanderthal Man

A symposium was held to commemorate the one hundredth anniversary of the finding of human remains in a cave of the Neander Valley in Germany in 1856. This was three years before the publication of Darwin's *Origin of Species*. Actually, a skull of the Neanderthal type had been found eight years previously at Gibraltar, but was neglected.

Strangely, the Darwinians "were actually not very happy or enthusiastic about the first Neanderthal discovery" in Germany. The reason for their lack of enthusiasm was that these remains did not fit very well into the evolutionary beliefs of that day. The early Darwinians were looking for a living link between man and the gorilla or orangutang and were expecting to find it in unexplored tropical rain forests or among uncivilized human tribes. Idiots were considered significant as possible throw-backs to a type representing the form they sought in the natural state.

The capacity of the Neanderthal skull was too large, and it was questioned whether these people differed significantly from living men. One anthropologist compared the skull to that of a certain Irishman he knew. Similar types were thought to be observed among living European peasants. Even Thomas Henry Huxley, who was Darwin's chief prophet and defender, said the Neanderthal remains showed only a slight modification or exaggeration of the features of the Australian aborigine.

But the Neanderthal discovery could not be ignored, and the point of view among the evolutionists changed from the one just mentioned to that of considering these people low creatures of "gorilloid ferocity" with elongated and projecting canine teeth. That the teeth really were not so did not seem to make any difference. They were described as short of stature and walking with their knees habitually bent, and unable to stand erect. The neck was assumed to be thick and the head projecting forward. This description of the Neanderthals (except for the teeth) still is presented in some textbooks, although some outstanding anthropologists say the Neanderthals walked as straight as we do and may have been quite as intelligent as we are.

Two of the contributors to the symposium were permitted to examine the bones from which the description was made that greatly influenced subsequent writers and became the standard description presented by the textbooks. Although they were familiar with the literature on the subject, they said that they were not prepared for the fragmentary nature of the material, nor had they suspected the severity of the deformity caused by a pathological condition which existed during the life of the individual. Besides this they found errors in the reconstruction. In short, they concluded that the Neanderthal people walked erect, were not particularly short, and their heads did not protrude forward. They said, "There is thus no valid reason for the assumption that the posture of Neanderthal man . . . differed significantly from that of present-day man. . . . If he could be reincarnated and placed in a New York subway — provided that he were bathed, shaved, and dressed in modern clothing — it is doubtful whether he would attract any more attention than one of its modern denizens."

Another contributor to the symposium reported that in bones other than the skull, differences between the Neanderthals and modern populations are "much less marked than some writers in the past have been led to believe," and concluded that the skeletons are basically modern and that former views to the contrary are untenable.

Another anthropologist has pointed out that although the head of the Neanderthals is somewhat different in shape from ours, this has nothing to do with intelligence and we have no grounds for saying that they were inferior to us in this respect.

At one time it was believed by the evolutionists that the Neanderthals were ancestral to us, but later they considered it demonstrated that this was not the case. Now several anthropologists are saying again that the Neanderthals were our ancestors. Some years ago an author writing for *Scientific Monthly* said, "As more and more information has come to light concerning Pleistocene man, the problem of the Neanderthals becomes more and more confused."

27. The Piltdown Hoax

On November 21, 1953, it was announced to the world that the famous fossils found at Piltdown in England and long considered to be the oldest human remains, constituted a hoax which had deceived the scientists for forty years.

There were a number of reactions to this disclosure. One was the view that now Bible-believing Christians would have something to gloat over, but credit should be given to the scientists, for after all it was the scientists and not a preacher that discovered the hoax. But this is an altogether unfair attitude to take, for a Bible-believing Christian would not have been granted the least opportunity to prove the remains a hoax.

When Arthur Keith, one of the leading English authorities in this field, wished to examine the fossils soon after their discovery was announced, he was allowed only twenty minutes to look at them. The famous anthropologist L. S. B. Leakey has complained that he wished to make a study of the remains but was not allowed to examine them adequately and was given a plaster cast to work on. The Piltdown material at the British Museum was kept in a safe, where no one could see it.

Moreover, there *were* laymen who *did* declare the fossils fraudulent while the eminent scientists were making extravagant claims for them. Professor Weiner mentions by name four men who were not professional scientists who said the material was fraudulent. One of them, who was a clerk in a bank, had in his collection a flint from the Piltdown pit which he had labeled: "Stained by C. Dawson with intent to deceive." With it was a card on which he had written: "I challenge the S[outh] K[ensington] Museum authorities to test the implements . . . which the imposter Dawson says were 'excavated from the pit!'" He believed the important canine tooth found at the pit had been imported from France. Charles Dawson was the man who had told workers at the Piltdown gravel pit to look for fossils. It was in his honor that the Piltdown man was named *Eoanthropus dawsoni.*

The main controversy among the scientists was whether or not the jawbone belonged with the skull, because the jaw was so ape-like. It turned out that the jaw appeared ape-like because it really was from an ape, but the controversy arose because it was found with the skull and because the molar teeth were flattened in a way never observed in apes. The scientists did not notice that the forger had overdone it by filing the teeth too flat and removing from them an amount which never could happen in life. They did not even notice that the hoaxer did not polish the surfaces sufficiently and left tell-tale scratches from his file.

The canine tooth was missing from the jaw and the scientists described it as they thought it should be. The forger obligingly made one to their specifications and placed it where it could be found. It was a tooth from a young animal and was ground down much farther than would happen in life. In fact it was ground down so far that the pulp cavity was exposed. The hoaxer filled the pulp cavity with sand and sealed it up. This showed on the x-ray picture, but still the scientists insisted it was a normal tooth.

Then Mr. Dawson found a tooth and some bone fragments several miles away in a pile of rocks which had been raked up so the field could be tilled. No one thought it strange that a single tooth would be raked up with stones and this second find "confirmed" the belief that the jaw belonged with the skull, and many of the scientists who previously had doubted it now concurred.

The fact that the findings at Piltdown were proved to be a hoax does not mean that other discoveries were fraudulent also. But there is no need to dismiss lightly the gullibility of the scientists in overlooking these and other clues which attested to the real nature of the material. One cannot help wondering how much the scientists overlook what they do not wish to see in other evolutionary evidences.

28. The Brain of the Savage

Charles Darwin and Alfred Russell Wallace both got the same idea to explain how evolution could have come about. Both said they got the idea by reading the same essay written by Thomas Malthus, though some believe Darwin really got the idea elsewhere. Each developed the idea the same way, and the theory of evolution they developed was presented to the scientific world in the name of both of them on July 1, 1858. The idea was that since every species produced more offspring than can reach maturity, there is a struggle for survival in nature, and evolution has resulted because the individuals best suited to their environment tend to survive in greater numbers than those less well adapted to the environment. As new and superior varieties come about, this natural selection or principle of survival of the fittest favors the better types.

The two men did not quarrel over priority and they became good friends. However, there arose one serious difference of opinion between them. Wallace had spent many years living with primitive people and believed that the theory of evolution proposed by Darwin and himself could not explain the development of the brain of savages, for uncivilized people are hardly inferior to Europeans in mental ability. Wallace had observed that these people have much better brains than they need in order to be successful in the kind of life they live. He said that natural selection, based upon rivalry be-

77

tween savage tribes or individuals, could not have caused the evolution of such brains. When Darwin read a paper by Wallace which expressed this view, it is said that he wrote upon it a large "No!" and underlined it three times. He wrote to Wallace, "If you had not told me you had made these remarks I should have thought they had been added by someone else. I differ grievously from you and am very sorry for it."

Darwin's attitude toward the view of Wallace on this matter was based upon emotion and it was quite unscientific. Wallace was right and his criticism of Darwin's hypothesis never has been answered.

Professor Loren Eiseley, a scientist of note who is strongly committed to the evolutionary view, agrees with Wallace and says, "There is every reason to believe that whatever the nature of the forces involved in the production of the human brain, a long slow competition of human group with human group or race with race would not have resulted in such similar mental potentialities among all peoples everywhere. Something — some other factor — has escaped our attention." The factor which has escaped his attention and the attention of many other scientists, is God.

29. The "New Man"

The first sin of Satan was that he endeavored to be as God (Isa. 14:14). Later he enticed the first two human beings into sin by promising them that if they obeyed him they would "be as gods" (Gen. 3:5).

In recent times the public has been informed in several magazine articles how close scientists believe they are to achieving their goal of being like God. One author says that achievements are expected which will be so fantastic that it will be difficult to distinguish mad scientists from sane ones. Also he asks how it should be decided whom to let play the part of God when ultimate decisions are to be made.

It is said that sober scientists contemplate not *if* but *when* man will "control his own heredity and evolution." Men of science are struggling to learn how to rearrange portions of the genetic material, and "when that time comes, man's powers will be truly godlike."

It is believed that within a short time a woman may be able to go to the store and select for herself a frozen day-old embryo from a row of envelopes. The envelopes will be labeled so she may make a selection according to eye-color and other features which strike her fancy. This would not be an example of virgin birth, but it is postulated that actual virgin birth also may become common. Unless the principles of classical genetics can be circumvented, people produced in this way will all be females. According to some preachers, such people should not have a sin nature and in this respect be like Christ. The blasphemy of such a view becomes more evident as the practicality of producing people in this manner comes closer to realization, though actually it was just as blasphemous before.

"Education by injection" sounds like a blessing to college students, but misinformation could be administered as easily as truth. Brain centers could be stimulated to erase memories and to bring back forgotten ones, but by the same technique people could be made to think they remembered events which in reality never happened. This would be more efficient than present-day brainwashing techniques and the diabolical uses to which it could be put are obvious.

It is thought that the time may come when people can be copied and many duplicates may be produced of a single individual. Hundreds or thousands of copies could be produced. A prominent biologist has urged that now is the time to settle questions regarding the legal rights of such individuals so that when the time comes this already will have been done.

Some of these things go beyond anything indicated in Bible prophecy for the end times, and perhaps the Lord will return and put a stop to it before the scientists can go so far.

The author of an article quotes Jeremiah 13:23, "Can the Ethiopian change his skin or the leopard his spots? Then may ye also do good, that are accustomed to do evil." He boasts that it will be possible for us to change anything it pleases us to change. Then he seems to have a flash of insight and adds, "Then it follows — does it not? — that even we may also do good." He seems to realize that with all the certainty the scientists have that they will achieve their goal and play God, they still are not at all certain about being able to do that which is good.

It is shocking that scientists desire to play God, but it is distressing when religious leaders make such comments upon this as, ". . . should not the Christian welcome with enthusiasm every new advance that mirrors the Biblical vision of a kingdom in which 'there shall be no more death, neither sorrow, nor crying, nor pain'?"

Men think they are on their way toward gaining a position which rivals God's, but God says, "My glory I will not give to another" (Isa. 42:8).

30. What Is Man?

It is reported that L. S. B. Leakey, the famous anthropologist, said that either the word *man* must be redefined or else chimpanzees must be called men. The reason he made this statement is because it has been discovered that in their native habitat these apes make "tools." They strip leaves from stems and then probe into termite nests with the stems. They pull the stems from the nests and eat the termites which cling to them.

Dr. Leakey assumes that only men make tools, and further he defines stripping leaves from a stem to probe for termites as the making of a tool. Hence he arrives at the conclusion that either man must be redefined or chimps must be considered as one with us.

Some scientists have said that the Australopithecines, or "South African ape men," really were men because they made tools. But some anthropologists believe that these alleged tools were used *on* the Australopithecines instead of *by* them.

Benjamin Franklin said that man is a tool-using animal. This view of man was changed when it was observed that apes in captivity use sticks as levers for prying and they use poles to obtain things they cannot reach. Elephants use small branches to chase flies. A bird on the Galapagos Islands uses a twig or a thorn to probe insects from cracks in the bark of trees. There is even an insect which uses a tool, for a species of wasp takes a small stone and uses it to tamp down the ground where it has made a nest. Thus by defining man as a tool-*user* there would be real bird-men and insect-men. Obviously this would not do and therefore man was redefined as a tool-*maker*. As Professor Leakey says, if stripping leaves from a stem to make a probe for termites can be considered making a tool, then it is time to redefine man again. If chimpanzees suddenly became men by courtesy of a definition, it seems that consistency would demand that the other anthropoid apes — gorillas, orangutangs, and gibbons — also would have to be counted as men.

Actually this is much ado about nothing, or at least some ado about not very much, for all it shows is that these definitions of man are not valid and that they never were.

The discovery that chimps in the wild state "make tools" was made by Jane Goodall, now the Baroness van Lawick-Goodall. She went to their native habitat in Africa and spent months seeking and then following them until they finally accepted her and she could observe them close at hand. This was a brave thing to do and a very interesting experience. But the motivation for it was a belief that the study of the natural habits of chimpanzees could throw some light upon the origin of some of our human social practices, assuming that theirs and ours had a common origin. This is now the motivation for much of the research with animals, and, of course, its basis is contrary to Scripture.

For all their cleverness in fishing for termites, these apes are too stupid to take advantage of natural shelters, and they suffer miserably in the rain.

In Psalm 8 we read: "What is man, that thou art mindful of him? . . . for thou hast made him a little lower than the angels and hast crowned him with glory and honor. Thou madest him to have dominion over the works of thy hands; thou hast put all things under his feet. . . ."

This does not apply to chimpanzees.

31 Is Evolution Going on Now?

During the 1920's Professor Herbert Spencer Jennings of the Johns Hopkins University did some work which earned him the distinction of being called the first person actually to see and control the process of evolution among living things. He worked with microscopic organisms, one of which was a species of Difflugia. These creatures reproduce by dividing and so it is possible to obtain any number starting with just one. Selecting several characteristics, including size, he segregated the largest and smallest individuals in succeeding generations until he had a group of large creatures in which the smallest was larger than the largest in a group that had been selected for smallness. This was hailed as observing and controlling evolution, though the animals were still of the same species and they were not on their way to becoming anything else.

In recent times the work of Dr. H. B. D. Kettlewell is said to be the best example of evolution ever observed by man. In England there are several species of light colored moths which have a dark phase, due to a single mutation. In the old days the dark moths were rare. The light moths matched the trunks of the trees, where they sat during the daytime, and hence the birds ate the dark moths first since they were much more easily seen. Thus few dark moths lived to reproduce and the light moths predominated in the population. But since the industrial revolution, the trunks of the trees in industrialized areas have been darkened, and in these areas it is the dark moths that blend with the trees and the light moths stand out in contrast. As is to be expected, the birds eat the light moths first, since they are so much more easily seen, and the dark moths have a better chance to live and reproduce. As a result the dark moths have increased in the population. This makes sense, and the question may be asked — so what?

Dr. Kettlewell says that if Darwin had lived to see this "he would have witnessed the consummation and confirmation of his life's work." Now Darwin's life's work was to show that all forms of life on earth evolved from one or a few simple forms, so Dr. Kettlewell is saying in effect: It has been shown that Darwin was right — we did evolve from a simple form of life; it is proved because birds eat more dark moths from light trees and more light moths from dark trees. Actually it shows nothing of the sort. It is an example of a natural selection, the selection of contrasting moths by birds in nature, but it is not evolution. Hundreds of mutations are known in fruit flies and they still are fruit flies of the same species. But for one mutation in these moths the textbooks and popular magazines tell the public that now no one can doubt evolution for it has been proved to be a fact!

By such misleading information the public is made to believe that evolution has been proved to be a fact. It is based upon a false definition of the term "evolution," and it is like the case of the gamblers who say that everyone is a gambler in spite of himself because gambling is taking a chance and everyone takes some chances, such as driving a car on the highway. This is a false definition of gambling, but some are convinced that it is true — particularly those who would like to gamble. Similarly evolutionists are telling the public that everyone is an evolutionist in spite of himself, for evolution is change, and everyone is aware that changes do occur. Some are being deceived and are accepting this to be true, especially when those who declare this profess to be Bible-believers themselves.

32. Monkeys, Typewriters, and Shakespeare

There is a well-known statement to the effect that if a million monkeys typed for a million years on a million typewriters they might turn out a Shakesperian play. One version says all of Shakespeare's plays. Another version says all the books in the British Museum. These statements are intended to show by analogy that if evolution is given enough time it may by chance produce all known forms of life starting from lifeless matter.

If we assume some facts about the typing ability of monkeys, we can treat these facts mathematically and see how convincing the analogy really is. Actual monkeys would soon tire of typing and would pursue more pleasing simian sports while their typewriters stood idle through most of the million years. Therefore if we assume that these primates work diligently and find that they still are unable to produce anything of literary merit, the analogy will be shown to have no value. Indeed, the more extreme or absurd the assumptions we make favorable to their success, the more thoroughly the analogy will be discredited.

Instead of giving them standard typewriters, let us give the monkeys simplified machines with only capital letters, seven punctuation marks, and a spacing key. Let us assume that each of the million monkeys types constantly twenty-four hours a day at the speed which the world's champion human typist was able to maintain for a few minutes — about twelve-and-a-half words per second. The only other assumption is that the monkeys type purely by chance and are as likely to strike any key as any other key.

To make their task simple, let us see how long it would be expected to take them to write not a whole Shakespearian play but just the first line of Hamlet:

BER: WHO'S THERE?

The answer is that if this experiment were repeated a number of times it would be found on the average that it would take them about 284,000,000,000 years.

To type the first verse of Genesis, or something of equivalent length, would take them much longer:

IN THE BEGINNING GOD CREATED THE HEAVEN
AND THE EARTH

The length of time this would take is beyond our comprehension, but an illustration may help. Think of a large mountain which is solid rock. Once a year a bird comes and rubs its beak against the mountain, wearing away an amount equivalent to the finest grain of sand. (This is about .0025 inch in diameter.) At this rate of erosion the mountain would disappear very slowly, but when completely gone the monkeys would be just warming up. Think of a rock, not the size of a mountain or the size of the earth, but much larger than the whole solar system. Think of a rock so large, that if the sun were at its center, its surface would touch the nearest star. This star is so far away that light coming from it takes more than four years to get here, traveling 186,000 miles every second. If a bird came once every million years and removed an amount equivalent to the finest grain of sand, four such rocks would be worn away before the champion super simians would be expected to type Genesis 1:1.

All of this is fantastic, but one thing is clear. A million monkeys would not type a Shakesperian play in a million years.

Mathematicians have challenged the evolutionary biologists and have told them that the time which they assume was used by the evolutionary processes to bring about the living creatures of the earth was not sufficient time. Furthermore, evidences are accumulating that the evolutionists do not have at their disposal the great length of time that they think they have.

33. Darwin's Illness

For a long time there has been a rumor that shortly before his death Charles Darwin became a Bible-believing Christian. It is said that he confessed his conversion to a Lady Hope. Biographies of Darwin do not mention such an incident, and anyone who could document it would achieve something of considerable significance.

Darwin's wife was a Unitarian and was very religious. She deplored such of his writings which seemed to her to put God farther off. She attended church regularly, had the children confirmed in the Church of England, and read the Bible to them. She questioned whether it was right to knit or go visiting by carriage on Sundays. She had parts of Darwin's autobiography deleted because of their anti-Christian emphasis, though they since have been restored. In other words, if Darwin had professed faith at the end of his life, she would have rejoiced and would not have tried to suppress the news.

When Darwin was a young man he accepted the Bible literally, though there is no evidence that he understood the gospel message of salvation by grace. The only degree he ever earned was in theology and he planned to become a country clergyman. Concerning his intended career as a clergyman he said in his autobiography that the plan was never "formally given up, but died a natural death when on leaving Cambridge I joined the *Beagle* as naturalist." He called the day he sailed with the *Beagle* his "second birthday." During

the voyage he formulated evolutionary views, which reori-
ented his life. This was a tragic substitute for the second
birth of the Christian, being born again according to the
words of Christ to Nicodemus (John 3:1-17).

In connection with the story of his confession of conversion
to Lady Hope, it is alleged that Darwin said he regretted his
evolutionary views, which were the immature thoughts of his
inexperienced youth. This either demonstrates the spurious
nature of the story or else it makes Darwin a very great liar.
Darwin was fifty years old when he published *The Origin of
Species,* which brought him fame and has been given credit
for convincing the scientific world that evolution is true. It
was twelve years later that he published *The Descent of Man,*
in which he discussed human evolution and said that man
evolved from monkeys of the Eastern Hemisphere. There are
four volumes of his correspondence, plus other letters that have
been found, and he pushed evolution all his long life.

In his old age he wrote his autobiography, which he said
was just for his children, in which he wrote destructively of
Christian faith. Of his own loss of faith he said that while a
young man on the *Beagle,* "I had gradually come, by this
time, to see that the Old Testament from its manifestly false
history of the world . . . was no more to be trusted than the
sacred books of the Hindus or the beliefs of the barbarian."
He told his children that he lost his faith in Christianity as a
divine revelation because he found differences in the Gospel
accounts and because his observations of the laws of nature
made miracles incredible. He concluded: "Thus disbelief
crept over me at a very slow rate, but was at last complete.
The rate was so slow that I felt no distress, and have never
since doubted even for a single second that my conclusion was
correct. I can indeed hardly see how anyone ought to wish
Christianity to be true. . . ." There is no record that he asked
his autobiography to be changed.

Three years before his death he wrote to a student who

inquired about his religious views, "Science has nothing to do with Christ, except insofar that the habit of scientific research makes a man cautious in admitting evidence. As for a future life, every man must judge for himself between conflicting vague probabilities."

In the last letter he ever wrote, three weeks before he died, Darwin expressed the opinion that the origin of life would be found to be a "consequence of some general law," in other words, not through divine intervention.

Herbert Spencer did much to popularize evolution, and during his life he was acclaimed with greater praise than Darwin received. But when he died, he was refused burial in Westminster Abbey because of his anti-Christian utterances. Darwin, however, was interred there with honor. It seems that Darwin was just as anti-Christian as Spencer, but he did not express his opinions about religion publicly. At any rate, it was not because of a story concerning Lady Hope that Darwin was granted a place in Westminster Abbey.

34. Placebos

A substance which has no medicinal value in treating any particular ailment is called a placebo. This word has had a varied history in the English language for nearly a thousand years. It is from the Latin, meaning "I shall please." A placebo may be prescribed to please a patient who thinks he needs medication when he really does not, or it may be given to comfort a patient who is beyond help by medication.

The most important use of placebos in modern medicine is to test, by comparison, the effectiveness of medication which is believed to have real value. The placebo is prepared so as to be indistinguishable from the drug being tested, and those who administer the medications do not know which patients are receiving the placebo and which the active medicine. In this way an impartial survey is made of the relative merits of the active drug and the inert placebo.

In one study it was found that a placebo did just as well as a supposedly active drug in relieving patients who suffered from anxiety, restlessness, and irritability. This may not seem too surprising, since the nature of the disorder was largely mental.

It is more surprising to find that placebos may be effective in relieving real pain. Among thirty-nine patients suffering the pain of angina pectoris, as many were relieved by a placebo as by a drug which was considered to be a superior agent in the treatment of this condition. It has been found rather consistently that 30 per cent or more of the patients given a placebo obtain satisfactory relief from pain following major surgery. Various studies have confirmed the observation that the greater the degree of pain, the more effective the placebo is in bringing relief.

One half of the patients suffering from rheumatoid arthritis were benefited by a placebo — 12 per cent of them for longer than six months. Of the patients who did not respond to the placebo given in the form of tablets, more than half benefited when the placebo was given as an injection.

Besides relief from pain and stiffness, it was found that there was a reduction in the swelling among most of the patients who responded to the placebo.

This rather surprising influence of mind over matter may, to a certain extent, explain results obtained by practitioners of the healing cults. However, it must be kept in mind that a placebo is not a substitute for real medication. Someone has remarked about one of the healing cults that it is gaining ground — mostly in the cemetery. Another factor in which our knowledge is limited and which needs to be considered in appraising claims of the cults is the influence of Satanic power in mimicking the acts of God.

Skeptics have postulated that Christian prayer is merely a subjective experience, not unlike taking a placebo. An authority on placebos says that people who are benefited by placebos are characterized as self-centered, emotionally labile, habitual consumers of aspirin, and regular churchgoers. He gives no statistics to back this judgment. Another scientist who works in this field contradicts this opinion. He presents considerable evidence to show that there is no significant difference in the effect of placebos due to psychological characteristics of the people who are the subjects, nor to the scientific background or understanding of these people.

The life of George Mueller is just one outstanding example

among many which would need to be explained away by
the skeptic who holds that prayer is only a subjective experience. From personal experience, from the experiences of
others, and from the authority of Scripture, we know that
prayer is not a subjective, placebo-like experience.

"The effectual fervent prayer of a righteous man availeth
much" (James 5:16).

35. The Most Poisonous Poison

The most poisonous substance known to exist anywhere in the world may be found in preserved foods on the shelves or in the refrigerator of the ordinary home. The organism which produces this poison is common in the soil almost everywhere. It is a species of bacterium named *Closteridium botulinum,* and it differs from most disease-producing bacteria in that it seldom, if ever, attacks a person or animal directly. But under certain conditions it produces a deadly poison in food. It thrives where there is no air and little or no acidity.

Where foods are canned commercially the conditions are usually such that the organisms are killed, but cans of food never should be accepted if the ends are bulging from the pressure of gases within. The chief danger is in home-canned vegetables and meats. Canned fruits usually are safe because of their acidity, but contaminated olives, apricots, and other fruits have been reported.

The disorder which results from consuming such contaminated food is called botulism. This disease was first observed by physicians in Germany about 1735 as being fatal to persons who had eaten spoiled sausage.

Several strains of the bacteria produce somewhat different toxins. The one which seems to be the most common and which has been studied most thoroughly has been crystalized in the laboratory. Tests were made with mice and it was found to be so potent that an ounce of it could kill about 600,-000,000,000 mice. A report which gives some of the physical properties of the crystals states with significance that the taste is not known.

Wild ducks sometimes die by the thousands from botulism as they feed on decayed vegetation beneath the surface of mud. Horses and cattle can get it from spoiled food. Some animals which normally are not carnivorous may contract it from the marrow of bones which they eat because of a deficiency of calcium and phosphorous in their diet. Of all animals so far investigated, only vultures are immune to botulism. This seems to be a special favor granted to them by the Creator because of the nature of their customary food.

The production of toxin by these bacteria is such that a deadly amount is formed before the food shows any signs of being spoiled. Thus it is recommended that home-canned vegetables and meats be boiled for at least ten minutes before being sampled, as housewives have died from merely tasting a sample.

The only place in Scripture where the term "deadly poison" occurs is in James 3:8, where we read, "But the tongue can no man tame; it is an unruly evil, full of deadly poison." Altogether there are eight references to poison in the Bible, and half of them are associated with speech.

The most deadly poison in the world may be destroyed by less than an hour of boiling, but the evil effect of a few careless words can last for a lifetime.

36. Miracles

In this age of science there is an increasing trend not to believe that the miracles recorded in Scripture were supernatural acts of God. The tendency is to accept the basic facts but to explain away the supernatural aspect of the events and to replace this with a natural interpretation of what really happened.

Some textbooks of botany say it is generally believed that the manna which was eaten by the Israelites in the wilderness was a certain plant, a lichen named *Lecanora esculenta*. It is reported that natives of that part of the world still eat it during times of famine. Apparently this is sufficient to convince the uncritical that the Israelites ate lichens in the wilderness for forty years and that no miracle was involved. The textbooks do not mention that these lichens developed on every day except the Sabbath, and to compensate for this they produced twice as much food on the day before the Sabbath.

Some authors of books about insects are just as certain that the manna was a secretion of a scale insect, like *Gossyparia mannifera*, as the botanists are sure that it was a plant. They say that the natives still eat it and call it "man," that it tastes something like honey, and that it melts when the sun shines on it. This may convince some, but it is hard to believe that insects would observe the Sabbath any more than would a plant.

In her book about plants of the Bible, Winifred Walker ably depicts and describes these plants. But she says that the burning bush which Moses observed in the desert was not really burning but just appeared to be because it supported a parasitic plant that had red berries. She says that "it was not the bush that was burning. Rather the 'flame' was represented by a mistletoe that covered the shrub. It had berries, red, glowing, and transparent, needing only the light of the Lord Jehovah to give the appearance of true fire." This is a somewhat poetic way of saying that Moses was fooled by the sunlight striking red berries. She concludes, "When the audience was over, and Moses found himself once more alone, he saw that the bush had not been consumed." There is nothing miraculous about a burning bush. The miracle was that the bush was not consumed as it burned, and it was because of this that Moses turned aside to look. To avoid the miraculous and to support the berry version the author offers, she alters the Biblical account and has Moses observing that the bush was not consumed *after* he had turned aside to look and after his talk with the Lord.

A number of commentators agree that the most difficult miracle with which to deal is that of the coin in the fish's mouth (Matt. 17:24-27). Some allege that the Lord merely quoted a proverb to teach Peter that he should supply their needs by fishing. Others believe that the Lord intended Peter to catch a fish by hook and line to obtain the tribute money by selling it. Although the amount of the tax is not stated in the King James Version, it is stated in the Greek, and the amount for two persons was equivalent to the wages of a Roman soldier for four days. This much money could not be raised by selling one fish. One commentator mentions that a codfish caught in modern times had a watch in its stomach, apparently implying that for Peter to find a coin in the fish's mouth should seem to him, and to us, unusual but nothing more!

Many people completely miss the significance of this miracle because they think it was a Roman tax that is mentioned, and they believe that the incident teaches us that we should pay our taxes. However, it was not a Roman tax at all but a tribute paid to the Temple by every male Jew above twenty years of age. In the original Greek one reads that "they who received [the] didrachma came to Peter." This amount was equivalent to a half-shekel. It was established by the command of God to Moses and recorded in Exodus 30:11-16. Even the Emperor aided the Jews of the Roman Empire to convey this tribute money to Jerusalem.

Peter told the tribute collectors that the Lord would pay. But the Lord asked Peter, "Of whom do the kings of the earth take tribute, of their own children or of strangers?" Shortly before this Peter had acknowledged to the Lord, "Thou art the Christ, the Son of the living God." Thus Peter should have known better than to have expected Christ to pay tribute to the Temple of God. Furthermore, this tribute was a redemption for the soul, and no one but the only-begotten Son of God could claim exemption on that ground.

During the periods of time that the Jews were a subject people they were not permitted to coin silver, and therefore no shekels or half-shekels were available. For this reason it was customary for tw᠁ nen to pay their tribute together with one stater, a coin equivalent to the shekel. Thus the Lord told Peter he would find in the mouth of the fish a coin to pay the tribute for both of them.

The half-shekel tribute was a token of the price paid by our Lord on the cross for the redemption of souls. The rich were to pay no more and the poor no less, for all souls are of equal value in the sight of God. The Lord paid the tribute, though He had no need to do so, and He also paid for Peter as the representative of those who acknowledge Him as the Son of God. He paid the death penalty for sin, for which the half-shekel was a type, although He alone was exempt from it. He did it for us and for all who will acknowledge Him as the only-begotten Son of God and accept His atoning death in the place of the penalty they deserve.

37. Virgin Birth

Virgin birth, or parthenogenesis, is much more common among insects and lower forms of life than most people realize. It is a well-known fact that male bees, or drones, develop from unfertilized eggs. It probably is not as well known that the plant lice, or aphids, produce males only in the last generation of the summer and the fertilized females lay eggs that endure the rigors of winter. All the eggs hatch into females and the subsequent generations, until the summer's last, are parthenogenetically produced females.

There are some kinds of insects as well as many other lower creatures in which males are very rare or altogether unknown.

Parthenogenesis has been induced in some species by artificial means in the laboratory. Among the most noted cases are the silkworm moth, the frog, and the rabbit. The method used in producing rabbits which have no father presumably could be employed successfully in human beings also, but major surgery would be involved.

Although parthenogenesis occurs normally in many of the lower forms of life and can be induced in higher forms, it was quite surprising when the discovery was made at a Department of Agriculture experimental station that chicken and turkey eggs may develop without fertilization and without any laboratory assistance. Most of the eggs did not develop very far and few reached the hatching stage. For some time the record for longevity was held by a turkey that survived for twenty-two days, but later one reached maturity and reproduced.

This natural parthenogenesis among chickens and turkeys seems to have a hereditary basis as well as an environmental basis. It appears to be genetic, since to a certain extent it can be increased or decreased by selection of the stock from which the birds studied are taken. It also can be influenced by the environment because it has been found that the amount of parthenogenesis increased significantly when the birds were vaccinated for fowl pox.

In response to the publicity that followed the announcement of parthenogenesis among turkeys, a number of women reported bearing children that had no father. Most of these cases quickly were proven to be untrue and no evidence was found supporting the other cases. Skin grafts showed that the mother and child were genetically different. In cases of parthenogenesis they should be the same, as in the case of identical twins.

There are those who are quick to try to set aside every miracle of Scripture with a natural explanation. Even well-meaning evangelists have pointed to the case of the drone bee as an example of virgin birth in nature to make the virgin birth of our Lord seem more credible to unbelievers. But the things of God are spiritually discerned and seem as foolishness to the natural man. To explain away miracles as natural, or to make analogies between the supernatural acts of God and natural phenomena, is neither honest nor effective. It will not bring the non-believer to a faith in the Bible but it can injure the belief of those whose faith is not secure.

If human beings should sometime be produced who were virgin-born in accordance with the laws of nature — as a few rabbits in the laboratory — they would not have the attributes of Christ. They would not be sinless, they would not be able to make an atonement for sin, and they would not be a part of the Godhead. Some have tried to make a case that such human beings, with a mother but no father, would be sinless and essentially eternal. But as in the case of parthenogenetic rabbits and turkeys, they would tend to be unhealthy. For reasons which are somewhat technical, parthenogenetic birds are males, while virgin-born mammals and human beings would be females.

The virgin birth of our Lord was supernatural and it was different from any other birth that ever was or ever will be. He existed from the beginning and left the glories of heaven to become incarnate in human form that He might offer Himself a sacrifice for our redemption.

38. The Star of Bethlehem

There has been much speculation on the part of those who seek a natural explanation of Biblical events as to what the star of Bethlehem really was.

It has been suggested that it was a meteor or fireball, but this is not acceptable for these phenomena last for only a few seconds at most.

A comet has been another suggestion. Haley's comet appeared in 11 B.C., somewhat too early. The next comet to appear was somewhat too late. The exact date of the birth of Christ is not known, but there are evidences that according to our calendar it was around 6 B.C. As we will see, there are other reasons besides the timing why the star of Bethlehem could not have been such a thing as a comet.

Some favor the theory that it was a "nova" or a "super nova," a star which suddenly fires up to many times its former brilliance. Some have even thought the super nova observed by Tycho Brahe in 1572 was a periodic reappearance of the star of Bethlehem. But besides the lack of evidence that super novae recur, this one appeared in the constellation Cassiopeia, which is far north of the land of Israel. Others have questioned that an ordinary nova would last long enough and have pointed out that a super nova would have attracted sufficient notice that its occurrence would have been recorded in other lands.

The planet Venus has been given serious consideration.

Some have gone so far as to explain the fact that the star "stood over where the child was" by saying that when one of the wise men stopped for water at Bethlehem he saw a reflection of the star in the depths of the well and therefore knew that it was overhead and that they had reached their destination.

Since Venus is closer to the sun than the earth is, it always appears to us near the sun. Thus it never is in the sky long after sunset or much before sunrise. It can be high in the sky only in the daytime. It follows that if one of the wise men saw the reflection of the star in the well it must have been near noon at a time when the planet was as far north as it can go. The extreme northern limit of Venus is about twenty-four degrees north latitude, the latitude of Aswan in Egypt, now noted for its famous dam. The latitude of Bethlehem is about five hundred miles farther north. Thus Venus never could be directly overhead in Bethlehem.

The idea that one might see a bright star in the daytime in a well came from Aristotle. He postulated that a person down in a deep well looking *up* might be able to see a star in the daytime, as the well would cut out some of the sun's light. There is no reason to believe a person could see the reflection of a star while looking *down* into a well under any circumstances.

The favored theory is that the star of Bethlehem was the apparent close approach of two or three planets. John Kepler figured out that there was such an approach of Jupiter and Saturn at about the right time. Later investigations have revealed that at their closest approach on this occasion they were about as far apart as twice the apparent diameter of the moon, and thus they by no means looked like a single star. The following year these two slowly moving planets were joined by the rapidly moving Mars, forming a triangle. But subsequent calculations have shown that they were so near the sun at this time that they could not have been observed.

Even if one does accept such a conjunction of planets as "a star," there still remains the fact that they would not disappear and reappear and direct men to a particular place, remaining over it as a marker. As all natural explanations fail, the only answer remaining is that this phenomenon was a supernatural one. It seems comparable to the Shekinah Glory which led the Israelites as a pillar of fire in the wilderness and stood over the Tabernacle as a cloud.

39. Darkness at Noonday

On the day of the crucifixion there was darkness upon the earth from about noon till three in the afternoon. A number of modern translations of Luke's account say that the darkness was due to an eclipse of the sun. A natural explanation of this kind is altogether impossible for two reasons. In the first place, the longest possible time that darkness can result from an eclipse of the sun is about seven and a half minutes, while this darkness lasted for three hours. In the second place, the crucifixion occurred at the time of the Passover, which was at the time of full moon. An eclipse of the sun takes place when the moon passes in front of the sun, temporarily obscuring its light. Thus the sun and the moon appear to occupy the same position in the sky. But when the moon is full it is in the opposite side of the sky, as far from the sun as possible, and at this time it rises as the sun sets.

Since the darkness could not have been caused by an eclipse and since this is well known in modern times, it seems to follow that some translators think Luke made a mistake and that they can best translate his statement into modern language by saying he attributed it to an eclipse. We cannot be positive about Luke's knowledge of eclipses, but beside the fact that the Bible was written under the inspiration of God, the true nature of eclipses was known before the time of Luke. Luke was a physician, an educated person.

The Roman poet Ennius is said to have described the eclipse of June 21, 400 B.C., in the following words: "On the Nones

106

of June the sun was covered by the moon and night." As early as 500 B.C. the relative motions of the sun and moon were known with great accuracy in Babylonia.

Thayer's Lexicon says the verb used here can *perhaps* refer to an eclipse but is intransitive and that in this case the reading is without doubt, ". . . the sun having failed." A. T. Robertson (*Word Pictures in the New Testament*) says that the Revised Version (of 1881) translates the word correctly, ". . . the sun's light failing," leaving the cause unexplained. Moulton and Milligan (*The Vocabulary of the Greek Testament*) make a study of the contemporary usage of words from Egyptian papyri and conclude, ". . . it seems more than doubtful that in Luke 23:45 any reference is intended to an eclipse."

There has been much discussion about whether the darkness was world wide or local. Some believe the language is ambiguous on this point while others say the structure of the sentence shows that reference is made to the whole earth. In this regard Origen refers to some remarks about an eclipse by a heathen named Phlegon, but it seems most likely that he was writing about a real eclipse in Bithynia. Tertullian, in the twenty-first chapter of his apology, written to the Roman authorities, said the following, according to a rather recent translation by Rudolph Arbesmann *et al* (*Apologetical Works*): ". . . although the sun was in the midst of her course, the daylight disappeared. Those that did not know that this, too, had been foretold of Christ thought that there was merely an eclipse. Yet, you have this disappearance of the sun all over the world related in your own archives."

The evidence compels the conclusion that there was a great unexplained supernatural event. While the Maker of the universe and Lord of creation suffered horrible torture and humiliation nailed to a cross between two criminals, the sun's light failed and darkness descended as He laid down His life in atonement for the sins of the world.

40. Jonah

The history of Jonah is one of the areas of the Bible most used by the critics in an effort to discredit the sacred text. It is stated repeatedly that a large whale has a small gullet and would have difficulty swallowing an object as large as an orange. The orange seems to be a favorite example of what a whale cannot swallow. Years ago a man had an exhibit of an embalmed whale on a railroad flatcar, and he also impressed the local people where his exhibit stopped by telling them it could not have swallowed an orange.

There are two groups of whales, the toothed whales and the baleen or whalebone whales. The latter have in their mouths strainers made of the baleen. Their food is plankton, the floating creatures of the sea that are carried by the currents. Most of them are small and many are microscopic. The blue whale, the largest of all the whales, is of this type. It may reach a hundred feet in length, but with its baleen strainer and small gullet it cannot ingest anything large.

The sperm whale reaches a length of about sixty-three feet. It is a toothed whale and has no baleen and it is not restricted to a diet of small objects. In fact, one of its foods is the giant squid of the ocean depths, the largest of all the invertebrate animals. The body of the giant squid may be as much as twenty feet long and its tentacles, as thick as a man's leg, can reach a length of thirty feet or more. A sperm whale could very easily swallow a man, and dying whales have regurgitated chunks of food which were larger than the body of a man.

There is the frequently mentioned case of James Bartley, a whaler on the ship *Star of the East*. In February of 1891 he was in a small boat with other whalers pursuing a sperm whale. The harpooned whale destroyed the boat with a stroke of its tail. All the men were rescued except two. The body of one man was recovered but there was no sign of James Bartley. When the whale was cut open, he was found inside, unconscious but still alive. He recovered but his skin was permanently marked by the digestive juices of the whale.

Also there are sharks that can swallow a man and they have been known to swallow a horse and a deer. In the year 1758 a sailor fell overboard in the Mediterranean and was seen taken by a large shark. The captain shot the shark and the sailor was recovered alive.

Some point out an apparent contradiction in that in the Old Testament the creature is called a fish, while in the New Testament it is referred to as a whale. A whale is not a fish. But in any case of disputed meanings of words in a translation it is essential to examine the words in the language of the original text. It is found that in the original these words refer to a creature of the sea and do not distinguish between whale and fish. In olden times people were not concerned with the details of classification which intrigue modern biologists. Actually, some classifiers do not include the sharks among the fish. Sharks do not have bones, and they also differ from typical fish in other ways. A shark is an elasmobranch, and some taxonomists do not classify these as fish.

Jonah was a type of the Lord Jesus Christ. He was inside the sea creature three days and three nights and came out alive, as Christ arose after three days and three nights in the tomb (Matthew 12:40). A whale can swallow a man and so can a shark. Whatever it was in the case of Jonah, it was something that the Lord *prepared* (Jonah 1:17), and that he came out alive after so long a time is a miracle.

41. The Yule Log

About the beginning of the fourth century, the twenty-fifth of December was adopted as the date of Christ's birth. The pagans of Europe and the British Isles observed the birthday of the sun god on this day, and it was thought that the heathen could be induced more easily to divert their worship from the sun god to Christ if the birth of Christ were celebrated on the same day. But this was not successful. Those who come to Christ must have as their motivation love and loyalty to Him. Compromising with heathenism only brings pagan practices and doctrines into Christian worship.

In the unfortunate amalgamism of paganism and Christianity which resulted from the selection of this day for the observance of the birth of Christ, the ceremonial fires which had been built in worship of the sun god continued as the burning of the yule log. Among the various superstitions associated with the yule log which continued until recent times were beliefs that its ashes kept in the house afforded protection from burglars as well as from witches and evil spirits, prevented toothaches, cured tuberculosis, healed swollen glands, and drove out vermin. In almost every country where the yule log was burned, people believed that remains from it protected from fire and especially from lightning. It is believed that this superstition came about because the yule log usually was oak, and the oak tree was sacred to the thunder god.

In some places it was thought that before the log was burned, the virgin Mary holding the infant Jesus sat upon it invisibly. The hinges of doors were greased so they would not make a noise to disturb the sleeping infant while the log was in the house before it was burned in the fireplace. For a person to sit on the log was an act of disrespect which would be punished with an attack of boils, and this could be cured only if the person passed nine times under a bramble bush.

In parts of southeastern Europe until recently (the Communists put a stop to it) the tree selected for the yule log was greeted with the words, "Happy Yuletide to you!" It was cut so as to fall to the east just as the sun was rising — another reminder that the custom arose from sun worship. Children went from house to house singing songs in which the pagan deity Colleda was invoked in prayer in every line. As the yule log was brought in, the head of the house greeted it as a person, drank to its health, and placed it in the fire. As the customary ritual continued, the mother scattered straw around the floor while making a noise like a hen and the children followed, making sounds like chicks. The father threw walnuts into the corners in the name of the Holy Trinity and prayed to the Christian God for the health, happiness, and prosperity of the family.

But God will not be mocked in this manner. He has said: "I am the Lord: That is my name: and my glory I will not give to another, neither my praise to graven images" (Isa. 42:8). Also the Lord Jesus Christ will not share His position with pagan deities or rituals. He said: "I am the way, the truth, and the life: no man cometh unto the Father but by me" (John 14:6).

We may think that we are beyond being influenced by heathen customs, but everything that detracts from the glory and honor due to Christ is of this nature.

42. Extra Sensory Perception

There is a persistent controversy about ESP, or extra sensory perception. This is the ability to perceive things without employing the known senses, such as sight, touch, and hearing. Those who engage in research in this area have made their experimental methods more and more rigorous in an effort to silence all critics who allege fraud. For some time they have taken the position that ESP has been proven to be a fact which needs no further demonstration, and that therefore present and future research in this area should be directed toward investigating the nature of the phenomenon itself.

Experiments designed to demonstrate the ability of some people to perceive beyond their physical senses include such things as listing in order the figures on a stack of cards in the dark, or on cards which are in another building which may be several feet or some miles away. A buzzer system is used to indicate when the subject has recorded the figure on a card and it is time for a co-worker in the other building to look at the next card, and if possible to transmit by extra sensory means the figure upon it to the mind of the other person.

Some scientists will not accept ESP as a fact, no matter how strong the evidence. An example of this is Dr. George R. Price of the University of Minnesota, who admits there is very strong evidence of ESP. He says, "Against all this evidence, almost the only defense remaining to the skeptical scientist is ignorance, ignorance concerning the work itself and concerning its implications." He sees that ESP and science are incompatible and believes that it is necessary to reject one or the other. Therefore, in spite of the strong evidence which he recognizes in favor of ESP, he rejects ESP because he prefers to reject it instead of science.

During June of 1965 a seminar on ESP was held at the University of California at Los Angeles. In this highly respectable academic environment ESP was accepted as a fact, and the chief concern was the continuing search for an explanation of the phenomenon. It is quite significant that the researchers decided not to limit themselves strictly to ESP but also to consider in their investigation the phenomena of spiritism. This indeed may be the clue to the answer for which they are looking and which to date they have not recognized.

When it is genuine and not fraudulent, spiritism is based upon the activities of demons, or evil spirits. The Bible says that this is an abomination to the Lord and it is forbidden to His people. If the phenomena of ESP are associated with spiritism then Bible-believing Christians should have nothing to do with ESP. Furthermore, if ESP is associated with the phenomena of spiritism, then ESP never can be put on a scientific basis. The scientific method depends upon repeatability — under the same circumstances the same cause will always produce the same effect. But demons have wills of their own and under the same circumstances they will not necessarily always react the same way.

The reader will find in a book about ESP by Susy Smith, who is said to be an authority in this field, that discussions of ESP shift easily into discussions of the phenomena of spiritism and back again. She calls psychokinesis (the influence of mind over matter) the Siamese twin of ESP and says they are so much alike that often they are distinguished only with pedantic exactitude. This includes the power some people claim they have to make dice fall a certain way more frequently than they would by chance. It also includes the influence of "unknown psychic powers" over material objects. This influence is exhibited when chairs move for no observable reason or when dishes fly across a room. These and similar phenomena have been reported many times.

It seems that nearly everyone at some time or other has had an experience which seems beyond natural explanation, such as a foreboding about something happening at a distance which later was verified to be a fact. Having such experiences should not be encouraged. If they come from an evil source, much more harm than good comes from developing them. If they come from the Lord, then as we are committed to Him there is no need to develop such powers. There are on record many cases where people have been led by a strong urge to do something unusual to help someone else, and to find later that it was the direct answer to the other person's prayer to the Lord for a particular need. Similarly there are cases where people have felt a strong urge to pray for someone, and later to find that the person was in grave danger at the time.

There is no reason to believe that the Lord would help people to do such things as are attempted in tests with ESP, such as calling the order of cards in a stack more accurately than would be done by chance. Especially, there is no reason to believe the Lord would help people do such things when they are not committed to Him. All indications are that Christian people should have nothing to do with experiments involving ESP.

The only proper contact with the supernatural for the Christian is prayer to God in Christ's name.

43. Mathematics and Scripture

The fact that there are mathematicians who are not Christians in a land where the Bible is well known, shows that one cannot prove mathematically that the Bible is the Word of God. At least part of the explanation of this is the fact that head knowledge is not enough. As an illustration we may cite the case of Israel at Mount Sinai. Although they had experienced many supernatural manifestations of the work of God in their behalf and at the very time they knew Moses was representing them in the presence of God, they made a calf of gold and said, "This is what brought us out of Egypt."

One of the aspects of Scripture which most readily lends itself to mathematical treatment is prophecy. To evaluate mathematically the evidence of prophecy one needs to know just two things: the number of prophecies and the probability of each being fulfilled. If we use figures which are much more conservative than they need to be and still find the evidence to be very great, the value of the evidence thereby should be demonstrated to be overwhelming.

Not all prophecies will be accepted as such by non-believers. The prophecies of Daniel 11, for example, are so remarkable that the skeptics think they must have been written after the events they describe. Some scholarly theologians do not accept the prophecy of the virgin birth of Christ although: (1) the rabbis before the time of Christ taught that this prophecy revealed that the Messiah would be virgin-born, (2) the Septuagint translation of the third century before Christ states it clearly in the Greek, (3) the New Testament plainly says that Christ was virgin-born and that it had been so prophesied.

Let us consider only the prophecies of the Old Testament which were fulfilled in Christ while He was upon the earth. There are over a hundred of these. It is difficult to assign a probability to the fulfillment of each prophecy in an imposter, but as a conservative estimate we may take an equal probability of it being fulfilled or not fulfilled. If these two statements are accepted, a simple mathematical procedure will tell what the probability is that all the prophecies would be fulfilled in an imposter. For one hundred prophecies, the probability is less than one chance in 1,000,000,000,000,000,-000,000,000,000,000.

This figure is incomprehensible to us. To make it more understandable we may make an illustration. If we have a mass of beans and one bean is a different color from the rest, then the chance of ninety-two prophecies being fulfilled in an imposter is equivalent to the chance of a blindfolded person picking the bean of a different color from a mass of beans the size of the earth. For ninety-three prophecies the mass of beans would be twice the size of the earth. For ninety-four prophecies it would be four times the size of the earth, and so forth.

Thus we must conclude that the prophecies fulfilled in Christ could not have been fulfilled in anyone else. Never did anyone have better credentials.

Besides the evidence of the prophecies there are other evidences that Christ is the One He claimed to be. The miracles are evidences. There are the testimonies of contemporary witnesses and His testimony of Himself. No doubt the greatest evidence of all is His resurrection after three days from a sealed and guarded tomb.

After His resurrection the Lord appeared to more than five hundred people at one time. But some will not believe no matter how strong the evidence is. The disciple Thomas at first would not believe Christ arose, but when he saw for himself he could no longer doubt. The Lord's comment to Thomas was, "Blessed are they that have not seen, and yet have believed" (John 20:29).

44. Cooperation in Nature

If flatworms are irradiated with ultraviolet light they die. However, if a number are kept together after this treatment they do not die as soon as they would if they were separated and kept in isolation.

An ant working on a nest will move more earth when working with other ants than when working alone.

When the tail of a tadpole is cut off it will regenerate more rapidly if the tadpole is among other tadpoles than if it is kept alone. Some believe the other tadpoles raise the salt concentration of the water and thus afford a beneficial influence. This theory could be tested by keeping the tadpoles in running water, where salts could not accumulate.

Sea gulls in a large flock produce more offspring on the average than sea gulls in a small flock.

White mice raised several to a cage develop faster than white mice raised in isolation. It has been suggested that those raised together keep each other warm and thus conserve energy for growth. Raising the mice at a temperature where they would have no need to keep each other warm would test this theory.

Many other examples could be given to illustrate a benefit which animals receive from their fellows through harmonious association. Whether or not one can find out a reason or reasons for this, the fact remains.

African elephants have been seen to aid a wounded member, though it involved much effort, instead of abandoning him and seeking safety for themselves.

A dolphin that is ill will be held up in the water by others so that it is able to breathe.

A naturalist observed a jay bird in winter feeding an old bird which had lost the lower half of its beak.

No doubt the cases of altruism in the animal world which have been observed by man represent only a very small percentage of the instances that have occurred.

A number of kinds of animals will cooperate in defense or in catching food. Coyotes take turns chasing the same rabbit to spare their own strength while tiring the rabbit. Some pelicans group together as they come down on the water, and beating their wings they come toward shore in an ever narrowing semicircle, concentrating the trapped fish and ending with a feast for themselves.

When a sparrow took over a swallow's nest and could not be evicted, a large group of the swallows, somehow understanding their common purpose, took off and presently returned with mud which they skillfully used to seal up the nest with the sparrow trapped inside.

Even mutual aid between different species has been reported. From ancient times there has been a belief that dolphins sometimes come to the aid of humans in distress in the water. An instance of this was reported not many years ago when a dolphin was observed pushing to shore a person who was nearly unconscious. Scientists are reluctant to attribute purpose to such actions and postulate that perhaps the dolphin merely was being playful. There would be ways of finding out whether dolphins "play" this way or are being helpful to people needing aid.

As we have so many examples to illustrate how the Lord has put into the natures of animals, some of them very lowly indeed, to be of mutual benefit one to another, we should be duly shamed if we fail to heed His admonition to us: "Bear ye one another's burdens, and so fulfill the law of Christ" (Gal. 6:2).

45. Measurements

Suppose you make two marks at random on a smooth surface and then ask ten people to measure the distance between them. If all ten give you the same answer you can be certain of one thing — none of them measured very accurately. This apparent paradox occurs because an accurate measurement involves estimates based upon judgment. The more precise the measurement, the more difficult it is to line up the scale used in measuring and to estimate small fractions of it. If ten people all measure to the nearest eighth of an inch, they may all get the same answer. However, if they make a more accurate measurement — to the nearest hundredth or thousandth of an inch — it is not likely that all of them will obtain the same result. But even though the answers vary, they will be better than the answers which give the distance to the nearest eighth of an inch, and by a suitable mathematical technique one can ascertain which is probably the best.

Science has been called the art of measuring, and the progress of science has paralleled refinements in methods of measuring. In early times some of the standards of measurement were crude indeed. At one time the Jews had a series of ten standard weights with a mustard seed at one end and a citron at the other. It is said that in the first century A.D., to demonstrate the inaccuracy of such a system, Rabbi Akiva produced a citron so large he had to carry it on his shoulder.

In contrast to the crudeness of such weighing, there is in

the National Physical Laboratory of Great Britain a balance so nearly accurate that the error in its weighing is only one part in a billion. The person who operates it stands in an adjoining room and performs the manipulations by remote control while making observations through a small telescope. These precautions are necessary, because if he were closer, the heat of his body would cause an expansion of metal parts of the instrument and decrease its accuracy.

In scientific work the metric system is used most commonly, and its unit of length is the meter. A meter is the distance between two microscopic lines on a certain platinum-iridium bar when the bar is at 0° Centigrade and one atmosphere of pressure — plus some other specifications. In the United States the inch is so defined that a meter is 39.37 inches, but in England the meter is 39.370079 inches. Redefining the meter in terms of the wavelength of light at a certain part of the spectrum is expected to increase its accuracy nearly a hundred times above the previously maintained precision of an error of about two parts in ten million.

In striking contrast to the requirements for difficult and exacting measurements in science, those in our Christian life are very easy. Dividing by ten to find a tithe is one of the simplest of mathematical procedures, and a fraction incurred in figuring the tithe of any amount of money can be more than compensated for by the addition of a single cent. Beyond the tithe, it is best that our giving be so uncalculated that figuratively the left hand does not know what the right is doing. The followers of our Lord were told that according to the generosity with which they gave, they also would receive, pressed down, shaken together, and running over. Certainly there is no careful measuring here.

God loves a cheerful giver.